MAGA MINDSET

MAKING YOU AND
AMERICA GREAT AGAIN

Books by Mike Cernovich

MAGA MINDSET: Making YOU and America Great Again
Gorilla Mindset
Danger & Play: Essays on Masculinity

Castalia House Non-Fiction

SJWs Always Lie by Vox Day
Cuckservative by John Red Eagle and Vox Day
Equality: The Impossible Quest by Martin van Creveld
A History of Strategy by Martin van Creveld
4th Generation Warfare Handbook by William S. Lind and
LtCol Gregory A. Thiele, USMC
Transhuman and Subhuman by John C. Wright
Between Light and Shadow: The Fiction of Gene Wolfe, 1951 to 1986
by Marc Aramini
On the Existence of Gods by Dominic Saltarelli and Vox Day
Compost Everything by David the Good
Grow or Die by David the Good
Astronomy and Astrophysics by Dr. Sarah Salviander

MAGA MINDSET
MAKING YOU AND
AMERICA GREAT AGAIN

Mike Cernovich

MAGA MINDSET: Making YOU and America Great Again

Mike Cernovich

Published by Castalia House
Kouvola, Finland
www.castaliahouse.com

Editor: Vox Day
Cover Design: Ben Garrison

Contents

Introduction

What sort of madman releases a book about Donald Trump's campaign for presidency *before* the election is over? If Trump loses, you might be wondering, how will he make America and you great again? Those are fantastic questions.

But as you'll come to see as you read this book, whether he wins or loses, neither Trump nor the movement he has both inspired and ridden to the brink of the White House are simply going to disappear after November 8, 2016. Donald Trump has launched a peaceful revolution by becoming the voice for over 100 million Americans. Trump is following the American people as much as the people are following him.

Even the most ridiculously rigged polls against Trump put his support at 40 percent. Many polls suggest that as much as 55 percent of the nation supports Trump's actual policies, and that their main issue with the man is with some of his personality quirks.

Globalism, the destruction of the middle class, Wall Street's ownership of the federal government, and the wars against men and free speech aren't going away. These battles have been going on for years, and only recently have the American people realized how high the stakes are for them. It is not a particular vision for America that is at stake, but the existence of America and survival of the American people themselves.

MAGA Mindset is not a traditional political analysis of Donald Trump or the success of his political campaign, which would be boring and useless to you. Instead, this book highlights some of the cultural forces that have propelled Trump forward while using the example of his candidacy as a case study for your own life.

You will have a deeper understanding of America after reading this book. You'll also understand how truly terrible the media is, and you'll understand the reason for Trump's inevitable rise as well. And you'll understand why I was able to successfully predict Donald Trump would be the Republican nominee back when all the professional political pundits considered his campaign to be little more than a punchline for a joke.

Above all else, you will possess the mindset tools you need to succeed. Regardless of what happens on November 8, 2016, you are going to have to live your life. We can't always control the outcomes of elections, but we can certainly control our own mindset. And as the example of Donald Trump shows, he who controls his mindset controls his destiny.

We have a lot of work to do. No one said making America and you great again would be easy. Let's get started!

Mike Cernovich
Mission Viejo, California

Part 1: Culture

The media believes that Donald Trump rose to power and claimed the Republican nomination for President through his public speaking skills, his charisma, and the force of his will. But the truth is that his rise was inevitable, due to the media's stranglehold on American culture.

There are four engines driving the Trump train forward. First, Trump is a nationalist, so he puts America and American citizens first. Every other candidate in all four parties, Republican, Democrat, Libertarian, and Green, is a globalist who does not care about the United States and is unwilling to give any priority to American workers over their foreign competitors. No less than the Democrats, the GOP is characterized by a desire to change the essential nature of the United States through unlimited immigration. While many Republicans in Congress may disagree with that assessment, their failure to take any non-defensive actions has already spoken much louder than their words. While they have defeated amnesty attempts by both the Bush and Obama administrations, they have taken no steps whatsoever toward restoring America's traditional demographic balance.

Second, Trump has rejected the concept of white guilt. In the U.S., and throughout the West as a whole, whites are singled out as the evildoers of society. We've even seen social justice warriors claim that only whites are even capable of being racist, because "racism is prejudice plus power." That appears to be the only mathematical equation they're capable of constructing. They are certainly unaware of the historical one that states "diversity plus proximity equals war."

This societal disdain toward whites exists despite the fact that most cultures throughout history have committed atrocities far more intrinsically evil than anything whites have done. Moreover, whites were the first race to ban slavery, a practice that exists to this day in Africa, India, Pakistan, Saudi Arabia, and indeed, most of the Middle East. Forty-six million people are enslaved today, which is more people than the entire American population, black and white, when slavery was abolished in the United States.

Third, Trump is unapologetically masculine. For a society to function properly there must be a proper balancing of feminine and masculine energy. Masculinity and femininity are complements, not substitutes. Women and men are neither superior nor inferior to each other. We are co-equals who have different strengths and weaknesses. Women grow human life. Men support human life. But if one were to judge by the newspaper headlines and public policies, one could not escape the impression that men are evil and that woman can do no wrong. This is clearly not true, and Trump has unapologetically rejected the false narrative of the foot soldiers in the War on Men.

Fourth, and finally, Trump has attacked political correctness and the thought police culture. Indeed, the three paragraphs above discussing nationalism, white guilt, and men are themselves politically incorrect. And in defying political correctness, Trump has made himself politically bulletproof. It's hard for the occasional gaffe and or failure to perfectly gauge public opinion to hurt a man who is famous for being blunt and saying whatever he happens to think at the moment.

Nationalism v. Globalism: The Death of Conservatism

Trump's rise has been met with a chorus of cries that he is not a "true conservative", which is a charge that has been made about every Republican frontrunner since Richard Nixon, including Ronald Reagan. The once-prestigious *National Review* devoted an entire issue to complaining about Trump and attempting to rationalize Republican opposition to him. Titled "Against Trump," the issue primarily consisted of attacks from a broad spectrum of members of the conservative establishment, from pro-war neocons such as Bill Kristol and John Podhoretz to members of the Religious Right like Russell Moore, as well as media whores Dana Loesch and the mentally-unstable Glenn Beck.

National Review editor Rich Lowry described it this way:

> *We got a strong representative of the religious right—Russell Moore of the Southern Baptist Convention—and a dyed-in-the-wool libertarian, David Boaz of the Cato Institute. We pulled together popular voices from the Tea Party right, like Glenn Beck, Dana Loesch and Erick Erickson, who combine their powerful journalism with activism, along with editors of long-standing conservative magazines, like John Podhoretz of* Commentary, *R.R. Reno of* First Things *and Bill Kristol of the* Weekly Standard. *We balanced a Reagan hand present at the creation—former Reagan attorney general Ed Meese—with 27-year-old Katie Pavlich of Townhall.*

> —"Inside the 'Against Trump' Issue",
> *Politico*, January 23, 2016

What "Against Trump" and other conservative media attacks failed to do was define conservatism. No one has been able to explain why waging wars on foreign soils or increasing federal spending more than any president since Lyndon B. Johnson, as George W. Bush did, was conservative. No one has explained how socialized medicine, which Mitt Romney enacted as governor of Massachusetts, is conservative. ObamaCare is modeled after Romney-Care, for Christ's sake, but few of the same people attacking Trump hesitated before rallying behind Mitt Romney as the Republican candidate in 2012.

But the fact is that Trump is not a true conservative, because conservatism in the U.S. is dead. Since Reagan, when have we had a conservative President? Certainly neither Bush the Elder nor Bush the Younger meets the criteria. When is the last time Republicans even ran a conservative candidate for President? Neither John McCain nor Mitt Romney were conservatives either. And what has conservatism conserved anyhow? It has not conserved America or the U.S. Constitution. It has not even conserved the ladies rooms!

Trump is not a conservative. Trump is a nationalist, which is a loaded term that is worthy of definition.

Nationalism is a concept that is derived from the root word "nation". A nationalist puts the interests of his own country and, by extension, his countrymen, above the interests of other nations. A nationalist puts America first. Nationalists will work with other countries, but only when doing so is in the best interest of the United States of America.

You would think that the President of the United States would, by definition, be a nationalist. The nation is in the title of the job description, after all. Yet mainstream conservatives have gradually drifted away from nationalism and toward globalism.

To a globalist, Americans are no different than Nigerians, Mexicans, or Turks. Globalists believe that if someone in a foreign land is able to do a job cheaper than an American worker can, then those jobs should be offshored. According to globalists, Americans do not deserve to exist as a unique national identity, although it's another story for everyone else.

Globalists therefore favor open borders, despite the obvious consequences to the people living inside those "invisible lines in the sand". Globalism pushes Americans out of jobs at the lowest rungs of the economic ladder, reduces their wages, and imports criminality and disease. Yes, immigrants are taking the most undesirable jobs, but they're doing so at the expense of young Americans and the American poor.

One example of a globalist conservative is Marco Rubio, the darling of conservative elites, who sought to open America's borders even further.

As part of the Gang of Eight, a political alliance named after the eight United States senators who joined forces to push through an immigration amnesty under the name of "comprehensive immigration reform", Rubio also sought to increase the number of migrants from Syria from a few thousand to several million. That the migrants from Syrian tend to be overwhelmingly men of prime-fighting age means nothing to Rubio or other globalists. In the globalist worldview, America has no right to exist as a nation.

Trump rejected globalism with a powerful statement: "Build the Wall." Aside from the literal meaning of erecting a border between the United States and Mexico to prevent tens of millions of illegal immigrants, including drug dealers and Islamic terrorists, from entering America, the phrase is a symbol. "Building the Wall" is a powerful symbol of nationalism. It sends a powerful message that America has a right to exist in its own right. What is a nation without borders, after all? It is nothing.

"A nation cannot exist without a border," Trump declared. A nation is defined by its borders because a nation is its people. A nation is not a government, a flag, or even a state. A nation is a people. When you allow the entry of people who refuse to assimilate into American culture, or who outright hate American values such as freedom of speech, free enterprise, and religious tolerance, you change the foundation of the nation, and you change it for the worse.

At this point in time, most mainstream conservatives are globalists. They believe Americans do not have a right to exist as a people, and that America does not have the right to exist as a nation. Some may call that statement extreme, but if you refuse to define your borders or control who is permitted to immigrate to America, as they do everywhere from Israel to Australia, including Mexico, which deports more Central American illegals than we do, how can you possibly claim to be pro-American?

Nationalism works. Just look at another nationalist, Vladimir Putin, the President of Russia who has openly praised Trump. When the American media reported that Putin's approval ratings were down, keep in mind that they had fallen eight points to 82 percent! By contrast, Gallup reports Obama's average approval rating, for the duration of his term in office, to be 47 percent. Hillary Clinton's approval ratings are even worse, at 38 percent. The people of a nation desperately want their leaders to be nationalists; after all, they are electing those leaders in order to further their own interests.

Populism and the Free Trade Lie

Nationalism is the belief that nations like Israel and the U.S.A. have a right to self-determination, and populism is the view that a nation's domestic and foreign policy should benefit all Americans rather than a tiny sliver of special interest donors and megacorporations. Mainstream conservatism rejects populism on the grounds that billionaire donors matter more than ordinary, hard-working Americans do.

Conservatives preach that America, as part of a global economy, must support "free trade." Free trade is why mainstream conservatives support the offshoring of American jobs as well as treaties like NAFTA, the North American Free Trade Agreement, and more recently, the Trans Pacific Partnership (TPP).

Yet what they sell as "free trade" is free trade in name only. So-called "free trade agreements" consist of hundreds of pages spelling out highly specific rules and regulations that will govern over each nation's trade. That's a negotiated form of corporatism, not free trade. Real wages for American workers haven't risen over the past four decades! Real wages for American workers have barely budged since the early 1970s, with compensation increasingly coming in the form of fringe benefits due to rising healthcare costs.

Take the North American Free Trade Agreement (NAFTA) as an example. Five million manufacturing jobs have been lost since NAFTA was enacted. Now, some of those job losses weren't due to the agreement, because as the manufacturing sector becomes more efficient, employment will naturally shrink regardless. But all you have to do is type "manufacturing employment US" into Google to find a whole series of charts showing manufacturing employment dropping off like a rock from the year 2000 onward. Sure, many of those who lost manufacturing jobs found employment elsewhere, but almost all of them were found in lower-paying professions.

Think about that for a second. It's not going to be cost-effective for older workers who lost their jobs to pay for the education needed to train them for another profession, since they have fewer years to recoup their investment than younger workers. And while younger workers will be able to adapt to the new working environment with more ease, remember that we're now in an economy where a Bachelor's Degree is the equivalent of the old high school diploma, the bare minimum required for a job. Do you think that would be the case if we had more manufacturing jobs? Of course not.

Globalist conservatives and economists ignore this problem by claiming economic growth should be measured by Gross Domestic Product, or GDP. GDP is a measure of all economic activity, which consists of consumption, investment, government spending, and net exports. It doesn't take into account the way in which that economic activity is distributed across the population. Just because GDP is increasing doesn't mean its benefits are distributed evenly. If Bill Gates walks into a bar, the average wealth of every person in that room increases by billions of dollars, but no one has actually added so much as one single dollar to his pocket. Even Obama had to admit that 95 percent of the economic gains that occurred during the most recent economic "recovery" went to the top one percent of income-earners. The rich got richer thanks to his $787 billion spending program. No one else did.

How did that benefit America? How did that benefit Americans?

Similarly, government spending can artificially boost GDP when nothing of value has been created. For example, if the government spent $100 on a bagel instead of $1.50, that purchase would increase GDP by $100. If the government pays someone $15 an hour to dig a hole and fill it back up, that will boost GDP too. In fact, the more inefficient a government worker is at his job, the more GDP will be boosted. That's because, by definition, all government spending increases GDP.

As you can probably see by now, globalist conservatives do not care about American workers. They don't give a damn about Americans. To them, Americans are not their fellow citizens, but instead are disposable widgets to be used until broken. Even better is to never hire American workers at all, but instead offshore all jobs in the global marketplace to countries that lack the same level of rules and regulations that our politicians have imposed upon American citizens.

Unlike the globalist conservatives, Trump has consistently prioritized American workers in his speeches and in his campaign promises. "We will bring jobs home to the U.S.," he's said on multiple campaign occasions. Trump has even directly criticized U.S. companies whose actions have harmed their American workers.

When Nabisco announced plans to relocate a factory in Chicago to Mexico, Trump said that he'd never eat another Oreo again. When Disney replaced hundreds of American workers for cheaper foreign workers, Trump spoke out on behalf of Americans, stating, "I am calling TODAY on Disney to hire back every one of the workers they replaced." He continued in that vein when he took a jab at Marco Rubio for co-sponsoring the I-squared Act, which would have opened the floodgates to foreign workers.

Among the other keys to explaining Trump's inexplicable rise is his reaffirmation of the American identity. For decades the liberal bourgeois treated "American" as a bad word, and acted as if the nationalism it represents was akin to Nazism or something even worse. We are global citizens, they would tell us. Unfortunately for them, most Americans aren't buying it. No one ever really did, they were just intimidated into silence. If even powerful conservatives in leadership positions were afraid to be unapologetically pro-American, how could they speak up in defense of their nation?

I've always known this myself, having had grown up among those possessing a strong American identity and real sense of pride in our country. You don't have to dig deep to find articles that explain what Trump supporters like most about their candidate: they

identify with him as a "real American". They don't see him as a man-
ufactured, poll-tested puppet like Mitt Romney or Hillary Clinton,
an alien imposter like Marco Rubio or Ted Cruz, or a globalist sell-
out like Jeb Bush.

Naturally, many pundits took offense to Trump's triumph of
the American will. Among them is establishment Republican David
Frum, a "distant cousin" of establishment Democrat Paul Krugman,
who penned a piece following Sarah Palin's endorsement of Trump,
declaring her support to be "an alliance of the aggrieved." The article's subtitle described her endorsement as a "bet on the triumph of
identity over ideology." In the piece, Frum writes:

> What defined [Sarah Palin] was an identity as a "real
> American"—and her conviction that she was slighted and
> insulted and persecuted because of this identity. That's ex-
> actly the same feeling to which Donald Trump speaks, and
> which has buoyed his campaign. When he's president, he
> tells voters, department stores will say "Merry Christmas"
> again in their advertisements. Probably most of his listen-
> ers would know, if they considered it, that the president of
> the United States does not determine the ad copy for Wal-
> mart and Nordstrom's. They still appreciate the thought:
> He's one of us—and he's standing up for us against all of
> them—at a time when we feel weak and poor and belea-
> guered, and they seem more numerous, more dangerous,
> and more aggressive.

In fact, as Republicans in office continue to remind us that
they're conservative in name only, part of Trump's appeal comes
from the fact that he isn't simply preaching the same old brand of
Republicanism we're used to hearing.

Ann Coulter put it more eloquently than I ever could when she wrote, "Looking at what the party has become, I certainly hope he's not a 'real Republican.' I know he's a real American. Those used to be the same thing."

The War on Whites

As the insanity of political correctness morphed into its current form of militant social justice, the rules of the racism game were forever changed. As I mentioned previously, today's social justice warriors have gone through the mental gymnastics required to convince themselves that only whites are capable of being racist, and that disparaging whites on the basis of their race is not racist, but merely "punching up." This bizarre social justice privilege hierarchy is why today's progressives will blast a Christian for refusing to bake a cake for a gay couple, but remain silent when gangs of Muslims commit dozens of horrific sex crimes everywhere from Idaho to Paris.

Consider just a few examples. Jeet Heer of the *New Republic* asked Chris Hayes on Twitter, "I hate to be biased but what the hell is wrong with white men?" That sort of overt racism is gleefully expressed in public, as no one will face social censure or risk losing their job for attacking whites. But imagine if Jeet Heer, upon learning the news that blacks have committed a record number of murders in Chicago, wrote, "What is wrong with black men?" Such a statement would not only be widely condemned, but would be cited as proof that we live in a systemically racist nation.

Hating on whites is so common that it is now exhibited by the entire pundit class across the Left-Right political spectrum. *National Review*'s Kevin Williamson has published multiple articles that openly state white working class communities are indefensible and deserve to die. Consider the following quote from a Williamson piece that features a headline targeted at Trump, entitled "The Father-Fuhrer":

> *The truth about these dysfunctional, downscale communities is that they deserve to die. Economically, they are negative assets. Morally, they are indefensible. Forget all your cheap theatrical Bruce Springsteen crap. Forget your sanctimony about struggling Rust Belt factory towns and your conspiracy theories about the wily Orientals stealing our jobs. Forget your goddamned gypsum, and, if he has a problem with that, forget Ed Burke, too. The white American underclass is in thrall to a vicious, selfish culture whose main products are misery and used heroin needles.*

He's not alone in attacking whites and white communities. In defense of Williamson's words, David French, a conservative who also writes for *National Review* and briefly flirted with a Bill Kristol-endorsed presidential run, wrote: "These are strong words, but they are fundamentally true and important to say."

Hating whites has become a common, and accepted, sentiment in the media and among the professional political classes.

Donald Trump is the first candidate in years who has not only refused to attack whites, but instead chose to speak on their behalf and rally around their issues.

Jeet Heer immigrated from India to Canada, one of the whitest countries in the world, which continues to perplex those of us who wonder: If whites are so terrible, why is everyone trying to come to white countries? Here is an informative exchange on the subject between Gavin McInnes and feminist Heather Marie Scholl.

Gavin: The dominant narrative in America is white people are evil, white people suck, and we should be ashamed of ourselves.

Scholl: I don't think we should be ashamed of ourselves, I think we should take responsibility for the system we created.

Gavin: The best system in the world?

Scholl: We do not have the greatest system in the world.

Gavin: Who has a better system?

Scholl: There are plenty of European countries that are much better off than us.

Gavin: You mean the ones with a higher density of whites?

That shut her up, for the time being.

Even achieving the American dream isn't enough to shatter this anti-white mindset. Take Anil Dash as an example, a "social justice activist" who has repeatedly broadcast his anti-white racism, especially against white men. Dash immigrated to the U.S.A. from India, and has since become a multi-millionaire in the land of opportunity. It's a good thing he didn't succeed while white, or, according to his social justice mindset, his success would have been entirely attributable to his privilege.

The War on Free Speech

The social justice crowd has managed to openly declare war on freedom of speech without even touching the First Amendment. Take microaggressions as an example, a concept that restricts speech by putting political correctness on steroids. According to the social justice theory, microaggressions are "brief, everyday exchanges that send denigrating messages to certain individuals because of their group membership."

Of course, those "certain individuals" are limited to any identity that the Left deems to be "marginalized." Examples of such deplorable aggressions include asking people where they're from, telling foreigners that they speak English well, claiming to be color-blind, and using phrases such as "I believe the most qualified person should get the job," and "everyone can succeed in this society if they work hard enough." Yes, that's right, the American Dream has been declared to be a microaggression.

With a flexible and arbitrary standard of evidence like that, literally *anything* can be declared to be an aggression, and therefore a statement or opinion that justifies the speaker being silenced. We are informed that microaggressions can occur even if no offense was intended, and *even if both parties are unaware* that one just occurred. So, good luck self-policing your speech on the basis of *that* criteria.

Every sane American citizen is beginning to understand that our speech is being policed and that we have been silenced. Even Michael Bloomberg, the very liberal former mayor of New York City, went off on a tangent during a commencement speech at the University of Michigan in order to blast the culture of trigger warnings and microaggressions that is springing up around college campuses. As he said, "A micro aggression is just that: micro."

Even more dangerous than microaggressions is the fact that there are certain issues we are not allowed to talk about if we want to be allowed to participate in society, or even hold a job. Issues pertaining to race and gender stand out as the premier examples, as progressives will always assume the only possible reason for even talking about those issues is evil intentions on your part. Question the obviously false claim that one in four women are raped in college and you're "promoting rape culture." Point out the faulty math behind the gender wage gap and you're justifying misogyny. Question the outrageous declarations of groups like Black Lives Matter, or even speak out against their support for murdering police officers, and you're a racist.

And don't you dare commit the thought crime of holding an opinion while white.

It is not going too far to say that the new American motto is, "You can't say that!" And "that" is a constantly moving target, defined by the most radical leftists, who have managed to impose an increasingly strict politically correct culture on Americans. Their ability to adjust the narrative at will, and to always make sure it serves their interests, is because Republicans have allowed the liberal media to set the terms of acceptable debate.

We know, for example, that in the mind of progressives, white people—and only white people—are evil. You won't lose a job for saying you believe whites have oppressed minorities, even if you're throwing all white people under the bus for things that happened hundreds of years ago, things that every other race also did. While it's true whites have committed their fair share of bad deeds, it is also true that almost every ethnic and racial group in history has oppressed other groups at one time or another. Do we really need to remind progressives what race those running the *African* slave trade were? Would it be Islamophobic or anti-Semitic to point out that millions of blacks were enslaved by the *Arab* slave trade?

Let's look at something that is unquestionably true that you cannot say in public without putting your job and reputation at risk: "Blacks in Africa captured and sold slaves to Jewish slavers, who subsequently transported those slaves and sold them to whites in the United States."

That statement is historically true. It is easily verified. There are no doubts about it. And yet if a political pundit said that on the air, he'd be branded a racist and lose his job after a public display of faux-outrage. If you said that at the office, you'd be called into HR for a meeting. At best you'd be allowed to undergo re-education in a sensitive course. Far more likely is that you'd lose your job for creating a "hostile work environment." Note that the truth of the statement is totally irrelevant, because it's how the statement makes progressives *feel* that is more important.

If what you say makes them feel bad, then it's wrong. It doesn't matter if what you say is true or not.

Being silenced for telling the truth is a key feature of politically correct culture. As George Orwell famously put it, "Truth is treason in an empire of lies."

And yet, silencing hundreds of millions of people doesn't change their minds. It doesn't make them think any differently. It only makes them angrier and more desperate for someone who can speak for them. Trump has clearly recognized this, as can be seen in his constant attacks on politically correct culture. And needless to say, he practices what he preaches when it comes to political correctness.

In one of the first Republican primary debates, Trump was confronted with some of his statements that were deemed offensive and tweets that were said to be mean. And when he responded by saying that America has too many more important problems and that we didn't have time to spare for political correctness, the crowd absolutely *roared*. Americans are sick and tired of being silenced, and Trump is the only candidate who is unafraid to speak his mind. In a culture of imposed silence, even those who disagree with Trump's rhetoric can't help but appreciate the way in which he is unapologetic about saying what he thinks.

Many of Trump's supporters have said they don't care about his policy positions. "I'm just glad to have someone running for office who finally speaks his mind," is a sentiment that is commonly heard. Even Trump himself has said that his supporters don't care about policy specifics.

Donald Trump isn't afraid to speak out on issues that aren't politically correct. He has denounced the pay gap as a scam, admitted that lax border security has made America unsafe, and he has refused to accuse white Americans of being evil, racist bigots. Even though no one had ever accused him of racism prior to his run for office, his refusal to accuse his fellow Americans is enough to make him an evil racist bigot in the eyes of the Left.

Conservatives and Cuckservatives

There's a term that many of you have likely seen floating around the Internet at one time or another, but never seen defined: cuckservative.

A cuckservative is a Republican who enjoys watching his friends on the Right, and indeed, his entire country, get screwed over by the radical Left. The cuckservatives are the pansies who are happy to argue economics and foreign policy with the Left, but lose their backbones when it comes to race and gender issues. A cuckservative will never have the back of his nominal friends and allies, and instead prefers to join in the left-wing dogpile on fellow right-wingers.

A cuckservative will purge those the Left declares badthinkers like Steve Sailer, John Derbyshire, Ann Coulter, and RamZPaul from the Right without hesitation even though the Left doesn't hesitate to give left-wing extremists like Al Sharpton and Bill Ayers public media platforms. Not only that, cuckservatives unfairly attempt to delegitimize the valid points these right-wing badthinkers are making, and declare them to be "fringe" or "extreme Right."

Cuckservatives want to be part of the establishment. They take their lead from the mainstream media, as well as *Vox*, the *Huffington Post*, the surviving remnants of *Gawker*, and a whole portfolio of social justice-oriented sites.

A cuckservative spends massive amounts of time status-signaling and virtue-signaling to the Left. Cuckservatives feel the need to prove to the enemy that they're one of the good conservatives, one of the nice conservatives, not one of the mean, nasty, extreme bad conservatives.

A cuckservative sells out his allies on the Right by calling them racist as part of his effort to signal his virtue and good thinking to the Left.

A cuckservative cares more about attacking Donald Trump than putting any effort into understanding why Trump has grown a huge audience. Here is a hint: Trump's increasing popularity is not due to his policy positions. Instead, Trump's success is due to America's fatigue with cowardly cuckservatives constantly bowing down before the media establishment and trying to please the Left.

A cuckservative believes that Israel's border must be protected at all costs, but that even suggesting America has a border to protect is racist.

A cuckservative thinks that becoming a *New York Times* best-selling author matters more than making America great again.

A cuckservative lives in absolute terror of being called a racist.

A cuckservative calls people who use the term "cuckservative" racist.

And "Cuckservative" is an important book about immigration and America.

I wrote the introduction to *Cuckservative: How "Conservatives" Betrayed America*. It is a powerful and informative book. You should read it. It will open your eyes.

I used to be an open-borders libertarian myself. America is a great country, and I thought we should welcome people from around the world to live here and indoctrinate them into the American way. Keep in mind that this is still a position preferable to open borders liberalism, which welcomes people into the country without any attempt at assimilating them.

My view shifted radically over the years, as the idea that immigrants had to conform to American values came to be seen as imposing our cultural hegemony on them. Even suggesting that there is an exceptional American way is now seen as a microaggression, which is considered to be a form of assault by middle-class liberals who have never experienced an act of actual violence in their lives.

Indeed, according to the multicultural madness of today, there are no cultures that are superior or inferior to another. I wonder what those who seriously believe this think about the culture of the Islamic State, though maybe it would be a stretch to suppose that they're thinking anything at all.

I don't make this stuff up. If you say anything like this, then you have committed a microaggressive act of violence:

- "Men and women have equal opportunities for achievement."

- "Gender plays no part in who we hire."

- "America is the land of opportunity."

- "Everyone can succeed in this society, if they work hard enough."

I'm *really* not making this stuff up. You can find aggressive statements like these, and many, many more, in a list of microaggressions helpfully put out by the University of Wisconsin, among others.

Everything America stands for—hard work, perseverance, self-reliance, personal responsibility—all of these things are considered microaggressions by the Left. How can we expect immigrants to assimilate into American culture when the very ideas that make the foundation of our society are declared to be problematic and off-limits by the elites who are policing our every word?

Western Civilization is Under Attack

Western civilization is under attack and yet we have *zero* support from mainstream conservatives.

Republicans control Congress. They are the majority party in both the House and Senate. What have they used their power for? Are they advancing American interests? They call themselves conservatives, and yet it appears there is nothing about America that they wish to conserve.

Conservatives insist we open our borders to everyone who shows up there. They say that we must relax our standards, reduce our expectations, and change our ways on behalf of immigrants, which has led to poor rates of assimilation. Things have gotten to the point where *Mexico* is deporting more illegal Central American immigrants than we are. Guess what their justification is? Preserving Mexico's demographic balance, a justification that no American politician not named "Donald Trump" would dare to cite, lest he be branded a racist for life.

As you'd expect, Trump wasn't afraid to address the subject. In his policy paper on immigration, he stated his position very clearly.

The time has come for a new immigration commission to develop a new set of reforms to our legal immigration system in order to achieve the following goals:

- *To keep immigration levels, measured by population share, within historical norms*

All too often immigrants bring values from their inferior countries to the United States. And yet, merely saying that Western culture is superior is, according to prominent figures on the Right, racist, xenophobic, and bigoted. But even they must realize that those cultures are inferior. After all, immigrants wouldn't want to immigrate to our society if our culture didn't provide better and more desirable results.

How did I go from someone who hates writing about politics to one of the leading figures of the Right?

The truth is that I had no choice but to take up arms after being betrayed by so-called conservatives and others on the nominal right. No one would stand up for my rights—for our rights—as men.

Rather than have our backs, conservatives watched with glee while SJWs screwed us over repeatedly. The Gospel of Social Justice has been accepted as dogma and there are very few heretics willing to speak out against it.

Look at the issue of "rape culture", which is the insane idea that society actually condones and promotes rape, as an example. Not a single Republican spoke out against the hysteria of rape culture even as Barack Obama and the mainstream media promoted it. At different times, Obama has stated that "one in four women" and "one in five women" have been raped during their college career. Ignore the fact that both of those statistics can't be right at the same time and focus on the fact that if either statistic was correct, that would imply that American college campuses have higher rates of rape than the Democratic Republic of the Congo. Or, these days, Sweden.

This is obvious nonsense. 91 percent of college campuses didn't report a single rape in 2014. Are we supposed to believe that on the other nine percent of them, there are more female rape victims than there are female students?

But what about the possibility that campus rapes are under-reported? To consider that explanation, let's examine that claim through another lens. Vice-President Joe Biden tells us that one in five women are raped in college, and that only 12 percent of those rapes are reported. As Mark Perry of the American Enter-prise Institute noted, there were 98 reported sexual assaults at Ohio State University from 2009–2012. Assuming a 12 percent reporting rate, assuming that all of those 98 sexual assaults was a full-fledged rape, and that every assault, reported and unreported, was inflicted upon a different woman, that amounts to 817 out of the University's 28,000 students, which would indicate a four-year chance of rape on campus at 2.9 percent. That's shockingly high, of course, but it falls well short of 20 percent.

While simple arithmetic is enough to dispel the "rape culture" myth, it didn't stop the feminist fantasy from influencing public pol-icy. In 2011, the Department of Education sent a "Dear Colleague" letter to all universities receiving federal funding, which expanded Title IX of the Education Amendments of 1972 to require universi-ties to promptly investigate complaints of sexual misconduct and to sanction anyone found to have done wrong. In other words, it en-couraged colleges to establish internal kangaroo courts to investigate rape and sexual assault claims instead of having law enforcement ad-dress them. The justification for this was pure nonsense, as the letter cited the frequently debunked "1 in 5" statistic as its rationale.

The myth of "rape culture" is just one of many examples of Progressive advances against which many so-called conservatives refused to fight. Many men, and women too, sensed that we had been betrayed, although we didn't know what to call our new enemies.

Then, like magic, a meme emerged from the darkness. Like Prometheus's fire, it descended from the heights of Olympus and was given to Man to illuminate his way forward. This glorious meme was the word "cuckservative".

What is a cuckservative?

Ask ten people who use the term "cuckservative" to define it and you'll get at least 11 answers. Some use the word cuck to describe a weak man. Others use cuck to call out the type of conservative writer who is more concerned with impressing his friends at *Salon* than he is with taking a stand and fighting in the cultural war. Others use it to describe a general betrayal of the American people, particularly with regards to immigration and foreign wars.

I use cuckservative to describe prominent writers and talking heads on the political Right who are more concerned with being liked by SJWs than standing up for their actual allies. This desire to be liked and virtue-signal inspires them to let the Left screw over their own friends, and allies, and eventually, themselves.

A fantastic essay on the word by Milo Yiannopoulos, "'Cuckservative' Is a Gloriously Effective Insult That Should Not Be Slurred, Demonised, or Ridiculed", provides an excellent explanation.

It's easy to see why "cuck" makes such a good insult. It's a byword for needlessly relinquished manliness, for selling out and caving in. The original metaphor of watching your partner getting slammed by another dude now simply

means abandoned principles and a lack of backbone. It's
a byword for beta male or coward.

It is both educational and eye-opening to catalog cuckservatives in the media.

Did you know *National Review* has engaged in multiple purges of its top writers over the years? Yes, the once-great *National Review* has repeatedly fired its most popular writers, such as Joe Sobran, Mark Steyn and John Derbyshire, for offending people who don't read and don't like *National Review.* Even Ann Coulter, the author of 11 *New York Times*-bestselling books, lost her column at *National Review* after *liberals* complained about her. Why, you might well ask. Were they actually surprised that liberals didn't approve of the most influential female conservative of her generation?

This phenomenon is known as virtue-signaling, which Breitbart journalist Allum Bokhari describes as "pampered, hand-wringing brats using social media to look like heroes without having to do any of the work." It's a form of status seeking, but they are seeking to have their status raised by the enemy. These status-seeking conservatives work harder to signal their virtue to the Left than they do fighting for us on the Right.

Who is a cuckservative?

The cuckservatives came out in full force when Donald Trump began surging in the polls. Rather than attack the Left, they went after Trump. They portrayed him as a racist and called him a nativist just because he supported Americans.

When the conservative attacks on Trump began, my first thought was, "Wow! Where was all this energy for the last seven years of the Obama administration?" An outside observer might have imagined that the best way to energize Republicans is to have a strong, charismatic Republican run for office. But much to my surprise, they were not energized to support him, but to attack him instead.

Donald Trump was called a nativist for wanting to make sure that all new immigrants learned to share American values. His demand that immigrants learn English was deemed xenophobic. His idea of restricting immigration to only high-IQ immigrants was even deemed "problematic", a term commonly used by the Left. None of Trump's critics held Mexico, which deports more central American immigrants than the U.S.A. does, to the same standard. Mexico even justifies their immigration policy on the basis of preserving Mexican population demographics, but when Donald Trump even hinted at doing the same, he was lambasted for it by *conservatives*.

The demographic balance of America is one of the many things cuckservatives can't bother to conserve.

One cuckservative I've already mentioned, *National Review*'s Kevin Williamson, wrote an entire book devoted to hating on both Donald Trump and his supporters: *The Case Against Trump*. I'll channel my inner Trump here, point out that the book was a complete failure, and note that my previous book outsold Williamson's by an order of magnitude. The public doesn't think much better of it than I do, for as I write this, the book has an average rating of only 2.6 stars on Amazon and a paltry 31 reviews.

The fact is, Williamson is not writing what *National Review* readers or conservatives want to read. He and other cuckservatives like him are primarily writing in order to signal their willingness to be of service to the Left.

A cuckservative's audience is not conservative readers. Cuckservatives write for SJWs.

Read the excerpt from Williamson's book below and tell me how it's any different from the sort of thing an SJW at *Salon* would write:

> *It is therefore not entirely surprising that among Trump's admirers we find a substantial population of purportedly heterosexual men who praise their candidate in extravagantly gonadal terms—I will not bother to catalogue the examples of scrotal and penile celebration I have encountered in my desultory correspondence with the Trumpkins—while Trump's critics are ritually denounced as beta males, "cucks," or, in the popular white-nationalist phrase, "cuckservatives."*

Is Williamson a SJW or a conservative? Read more:

> *The Trumpkins savor the metaphor with great homoerotic gusto, proffering pornographic details about the prospect of fellating the black "bull" planning to ravish the white maiden of Western civilization. (One is tempted to offer to take them to a production of Othello.) I will note without comment that the sentiment "Donald Trump is a perfect example of an alpha male" is to be found on the comments board at—not that there's anything wrong with that!—BodyBuilding.com.*

That's not politics, that's pornography. There is something wrong, something *seriously wrong*, with cuckservatives. Like SJWs, they emotionally project their immorality and sickness on others.

Charles C.W. Cooke, a close friend and mentor to Williamson, is also a cuckservative.

Believe it or not, *Salon* actually published an article *praising pedophilia*. This is a glorious unforced error by our adversaries. When the Left openly advocates for pedophilia, you go on the attack.

What did Charles C.W. Cooke do? Did he rightly condemn this attempt by *Salon* to further push the envelope of America's moral boundaries? No! Not only did he pass up the opportunity to criticize the Left's latest lunacy, he actually wrote a defense of *Salon*'s pedophilia advocacy!

Incredibly, Charles C.W. Cooke, a nominal conservative, adopted an objectively pro-pedophile position. He wrote, "I've seen a good number of conservatives slamming this confession, often on the presumption that it represents an attempt to "mainstream" pedophilia. Respectfully, I have to disagree with this assessment."

He continues, "Naturally, I am as disgusted by the urges that are referenced in the piece as the next guy, and, despite the author's heartfelt plea for "understanding," I find it difficult not to harbor a real animus toward him. But I see no evidence whatsoever that *Salon* is endorsing or excusing child abuse, or that it is making the case that pedophilia is an "ingrained identity" and that its sufferers should therefore be free to act as they wish."

Of course, mainstreaming pedophilia by starting a public discussion about it is exactly what *Salon* is trying to do. Hell, *Salon* even tried to use it to score some political points against the Right with it through publishing a follow-up piece by the author-pedophile titled "I'm a pedophile, you're the monsters: my week inside the vile right wing hate machine."

That's right, opposing pedophilia is now intolerance.

If conservatives aren't willing to take the moral high ground on *pedophilia* of all issues, what exactly is it that they are willing to take on? What exactly is it that they are conserving?

The Allure of Trump

The media has treated Trump's policy positions and political philosophies as mysteries of the universe. This struck me as very odd, considering that Trump has posted over 30,000 tweets and has also written several books. His books and tweets were not referenced in any of the hit pieces on him. So, I started going over these tweets, most of which he posted before announcing his candidacy, to get a sense of his worldview.

Let's look at just a few of the clues Donald Trump has given us concerning the policies he intends to pursue as President over the years.

Trump was speaking out against PC culture long before he ran for office.

On December 5th, 2012, Trump tweeted, "I don't see the point of being politically correct if that means being incorrect."

Donald Trump recognized the danger of the cuck mindset.

"One point I made last night, and will continue to push, is that the GOP can't be politically correct. We must fight fire with fire." August 27th, 2012

Donald Trump has opposed immigration amnesties since 2012.

"Breitbart News continues to do great work in exposing the left-wing financing behind amnesty." June 3rd, 2012

"The new amnesty bill is over 1000 pages. It is another monstrosity ala ObamaCare." May 29th, 2012

"Amnesty is suicide for Republicans. Not one of those 12 million who broke our laws will vote Republican. Obama is laughing at the GOP." March 19th, 2013

Donald Trump does not believe America owes immigrants any handouts. In his book *Time to Get Tough: Making America #1 Again*, **Trump wrote:**

"Canada's legal immigration plan starts with a simple and smart question: How will any immigrant applying for citizenship 'support the development of a strong, prosperous Canadian economy'? Economic benefit should be our chief aim. America doesn't need freeloaders who come here to live off our welfare system. We need legal immigrants who bring skills, prosperity, and intellectual capital."

Trump opposed U.S. involvement in the Middle East.

"The Arab League stated that it wants nothing to do with an attack on Syria, but they want us to attack. Are our leaders insane or just stupid?" September 1st, 2013

In response to a tweet asking "How would you treat the Syria situation if you were President?", he replied, "I'd let them all fight with each other—and focus on the US!" September 1st, 2013

"President Obama's weakness and indecision may have saved us from doing a horrible and very costly (in more ways than money) attack on Syria!" September 1st, 2013

Trump does not believe the U.S. should continue to be cucked by Saudi Arabia.

"I just want to know how much is Saudi Arabia and others who are helping willing to pay for our saving from total extinction. Pay up now!" September 10th, 2014

"Saudi Arabia should fight their own wars, which they don't, or pay us an absolute fortune to protect them and their great wealth-$ trillions!" August 31st, 2014

"Have you been watching how Saudi Arabia has been taunting our VERY dumb political leaders to protect them from ISIS. Why aren't they paying?" August 31st, 2014

Trump was anti-establishment and defended the Tea Party against the GOP elite.

"The ruling GOP consultant class of losers like Karl Rove have no respect for the Tea Party. They do this at their own peril!" February 23rd, 2013

"I'm saying that the Tea Party, perhaps by another name, will soon have another big moment—and will be a major factor in victory!" February 24th, 2013

"Big response to my Tea Party statement—remember that they were nearly fully energized by Romney campaign and will have far more power with time." February 24th, 2013

"Republicans better start listening to and respecting the Tea Party!" February 23rd, 2013

Trump did not support the Wall Street bailouts.

"The banks need to start lending against otherwise the economy will continue its downturn. This is why we bailed the banks out!" January 31st, 2012

"The banks were bailed out by us. They should start lending to private entrepreneurs. The banks are slowing American growth." November 29th, 2011

"The Fannie and Freddie execs should not get million dollar bonuses with our tax dollars. They were bailed out with $169B of our money." November 10th, 2011

Trump has always put America first.

Back in 1988, a 42-year-old Donald Trump appeared on Oprah Winfrey's show to promote his book, *The Art of the Deal*. It didn't take long for the discussion to turn from business to politics.

Oprah made reference to one of Trump's first splashes in the political area, in the form of taking out $95,000 in newspaper ads attacking Japan and Saudi Arabia. He clarified that "we let Japan come in and dump everything right into our markets.... It's not free trade. Try selling someone in Japan, it's impossible. They come over here, they sell their cars, their VCRs. They knock the hell out of our companies. And, hey, I have tremendous respect for the Japanese people."

Swap out those names for China and Mexico and you have the same Donald Trump taking the same positions on trade we see today. Oprah replied to Trump "this sounds like political Presidential talk to me... would you ever [run for President]?"

"Probably not," he replied, "but I do get tired of seeing the country ripped off." There was one condition he would run under: "If things got so bad, I wouldn't want to rule it out entirely."

"I think I'd win," Trump said. "I'll tell you what—I wouldn't go in to lose. I've never gone in to lose."

30 years later, things have gotten that bad. And that's why Donald Trump is now the Republican nominee for President and the favorite to win the Presidential election.

The message the Right needs more than anything: think like a master, not like a slave.

National Review, like the rest of the mainstream Right, works very hard to renounce what is considered racism in a world where the Left has rendered the word meaningless. Although women are being raped in Cologne and French men and women are being mur-

dered in Paris, if you believe the conservative media, the real problem facing the world is @Ricky_Vaughn99 and his mean tweets.

Why does the Right work so hard renouncing trolls rather than
attacking the Left for allowing women to be raped?   David A.
French, a favorite of the neocons and a general of cuckmanship,
offers an indirect insight into the cuck mindset:

> *Calling out alleged "white identity politics" is an excellent*
> *way to avoid having to debate conservatives. After all,*
> *who needs to debate racists? As my friend Ravi Zacharias*
> *frequently observes—in the battle of ideas, stigma tends to*
> *defeat dogma. In other words, if you can shame and insult*
> *your opposition, then you never have to engage their ideas.*

Read that first sentence again. Frenchie is afraid of being called
a racist *by the Left* because then *the Left might not debate him.* And
if the Left won't debate him, then there go all those appearances on
the cable news shows and those gentlemanly we-agree-to-disagree
discussions with the talking heads of the Left.

Ponder what sort of mindset is required to cause a conservative
intellectual to live in sheer terror of being called names by people
who already hate his guts and despise everything he believes in?

David French and most of the conservative media has the cuck
mindset, which is a manifestation of the slave mindset. They are the
slaves and the liberal media are their masters. That is why they must
watch their words! If they say the wrong thing at the wrong time,
the Left will not debate them!

Meanwhile women are being raped in Europe. Muslims have
committed numerous terrorist attacks on American soil.   The
thought police have censored the silent majority of Americans. Soldiers are being killed on the streets of the United Kingdom. Young
men are being beaten up in Sweden. Concertgoers are slaughtered

in Paris nightclubs. Jews are fleeing France after being murdered by migrants.

Rather than fight for real Americans, rather than defend the West, David French and the rest of the cuckservative media will continue focusing on what really matters to them: people who post frog cartoons on the Internet.

Donald Trump and Manhood

The rise of Donald Trump in America and neo-nationalism across Europe demonstrates that the political landscape is shifting. Indeed, my own voice is rapidly growing more influential, as measured by any sort of metric of your choice, from website traffic, to book sales, podcast listeners, Twitter impressions, and Twitter followers.

Mainstream Republicans all know who I am, and yet they will not address me directly. Instead, they prefer to attack others like me for being anonymous on the Internet. They avoid even mentioning me because they are afraid that my influence will continue to grow. But they cannot stop me. It's too late.

After remaining happily apolitical for years, I've had to start advocating on behalf of men due to the changing circumstances today. And why is that? Because, today, if you're a man, *there is a target on your back.*

Don't believe me? Go get into an argument online, on any political topic, and see how long it takes before your argument is dismissed on the basis that you're a white male. It will happen very quickly, even though there are only two kinds of people who dismiss people's arguments solely based on their race and gender, racists, and social justice loonjobs.

We all know the Democratic Party hates men, but until recently the Republican Party was, at least ostensibly, not hateful toward men.

Yet despite the GOP controlling the Senate, not a single Republican senator spoke out against the aforementioned false rape hysteria. Due process protections are being aggressively eroded for men. If a woman regrets having sex with you, you're a rapist. If you and a woman have sex while you are both drunk, you're a rapist, because she can't consent while intoxicated, but apparently a man can. If only you could pull that excuse to get out of a DUI! "I'm sorry, your Honor, but I couldn't consent to driving the car, so obviously I can't be held responsible."

And guess what? There's not a damned thing Republicans will do to support men who are accused of rape, no matter how obviously ridiculous the accusation is.

Do I exaggerate? The *Washington Times* reported on how the Republican-controlled Congress is addressing the rampant problem of false rape accusations against men.

> *At a congressional hearing on campus sexual assault, Rep. Jared Polis (R, CO) suggested that expelling students based solely on the idea that they* might *have committed a crime is an acceptable standard. And the hearing audience applauded him.*

I remember learning about the Salem witch trials in middle school and thinking that it would be impossible for something so ridiculous to happen today, but human nature never changes. No one believes in witches anymore, and many are no longer deriving their morals from a holy book, and yet the witch hunts continue.

Rep. Polis went so far as to assert that the innocent should be punished along with the guilty. "I mean, if there's ten people that have been accused and under a reasonable likelihood standard maybe one or two did it, seems better to get rid of all ten people." So if you're one of those eight or nine innocents, you're just out of luck. So much for the judicial tradition of the Common Law, which famously includes the concept that it is better for ten guilty men to go free than for one innocent man to be jailed.

As of now, we men have no political support from either major party. In fact, there is no political party, or even political caucus within a party that is looking out for us. To even suggest that we might need one would be misogynistic.

We are on our own.

Or are we?

The New Right: The Ugly

Consider what I've been attacked by the many people on the mainstream Right for doing: going to the gym, having normal heterosexual relationships with women, and making a living by selling the books I write.

Seriously. To establishment Republicans, simply enjoying the company of women is vile.

Kurt Schlichter, a senior *Townhall* columnist, tweeted at me on September 10th, 2015: *"Your book was a yuuuuge success. Now do one of your sweet pick-up artist moves, player. America awaits."*

Another Republican falsely accused me of threatening him with rape, tweeting at me *"This guy (@Cernovich) is tough, people. And he wants you to know just how tough he is by threatening you with gay rape."*

The GOP has become feminized to the point that their attacks on me are almost indistinguishable from SJW attacks. What sort of people blatantly lie about easily verifiable facts that don't require any more research than just reading my Twitter feed? Social Justice Warriors, of course… and cuckservatives.

The Curious Case of Roosh V.

When Roosh V went on his worldwide speaking tour, he was physically assaulted in Montreal and publicly told he was not welcome in the cities of Toronto, Calgary, and Ottowa by their mayors, John Tory, Naheed Nenshi, and Jim Watson. If Roosh had insulted feminists to their faces or behaved like a boor, it still would not have been right to attack him, but at least you might understand how it got started. But that's not what happened.

Roosh insulted no one; instead, he simply asked people to respect his right to privacy and his right to free speech. Roosh intended to give a private talk to men who had purchased tickets to listen to his presentation. Is that too much to ask for? Well, as anyone who's ever attended a Milo Yiannopoulos lecture knows, the answer to that question these days is, without question, yes.

Roosh did not incite any attacks against himself. He didn't go out of his way to look for trouble. Instead, he took several expensive measures to keep feminists away from him, including multiple venues. He even hired bodyguards.

Roosh's life was threatened for giving a speech *in private*. Roosh was publicly denounced by government officials for giving a speech *in private*. Roosh was physically attacked by feminists for giving a speech *in private*.

What Republican had his back?

If a woman like Jessica Valenti had faced even ten percent of the attacks Roosh experienced, *Reason*, *National Review*, and every other conservative publication would have been quick to speak out. Just look at they sympathize with the Anita Sarkeesians of the world, the women who have made careers out of being professional victims.

Roosh's rights do not matter to them, because Roosh is a man.

The New Right: The Bad

There is a new anti-Semitism rising in the United States. As a member of the New Right, people ask me repeatedly to address this, as those on the New Right are often facing such accusations. This section will serve as my stock reply.

Whether someone is a Jew or not means nothing to me either way. I won't censor myself just because you are offended, nor will I hate you because of it. As Ben Shapiro likes to say, "the facts don't care about your feelings." I will treat you like a man regardless of who you are.

Yet there are many conservative political pundits who repeatedly remind others that they are Jews, as if that alone is some sort of argument. They claim any failure to support Israel is anti-Semitic, but are absolutely fine with openly attacking working-class men.

Kevin Eder offers one of many such examples. When it comes to criticizing liberals, he writes "Hi fellow Jews. Mr Obama just empowered people who want you dead with money and better weapons. Maybe vote a different way next time?" But then, addressing conservatives, he tweeted out a mockery of Donald Trump's campaign, likening it to the "They took our jobs!" character from South Park.

Are men really supposed to believe that liberals do wrong when they don't care about our international allies, but ignore the fact that conservatives do wrong when they don't care about us? When conservative pundits overtly mock the job losses endured by millions of working-class Americans, how can they possibly expect those same people to support their favored causes?

On what planet should white working-class Americans care about Israel? Among the old Right, American-Israeli loyalty was a one-way street, with working-class whites rushing to die in wars that were fought on Israel's behalf, while direct military attacks on Americans by Israelis, such as the U.S.S. *Liberty* Incident, in which 34 Americans were killed, and 171 wounded, by a combined attack by the Israeli Air Force and Navy, were quietly swept under the rug.

Jewish attacks on working-class whites have led to a lot of rage and anger. When you go around publicly announcing that you're a Jew, you hate white people, and you support the Third-World invasion of their countries, it's a bit much to cry about anti-Semitism and expect any sympathy when they return the sentiment.

Anyone who genuinely cares about peace should spend less time distancing themselves from imaginary racists on Twitter and spend more time calling out hypocritical media conservatives.

Here's an idea for Jonah Goldberg, Kevin Williamson, Cathy Young, and the many other right-wing pundits who clutch their pearls and shriek whenever they find themselves faced with "Nazi trolls" on Twitter: stop making racist attacks against white people!

Back in September 2015, Kevin Williamson described Trump supporters as "just a little trivial gang of gap-toothed peckerwood-trash idiot children cowering in anonymity on the internet." He followed it up by declaring that "the weird homoeroticism and sexual-panic metaphors of the Trump movement are remarkable."

As for everyone else, just ignore the trolls. Focus on the pundits. Focus on the media figures. It's the pundits, after all, who have the platform. They are the ones who need to watch their words, as the price of fame and influence is noblesse oblige.

When a conservative pundit says, "Let's all have a great laugh at the expense of Americans who lost their jobs," it's time to reply with, "You know, it's not actually funny that working class Americans are jobless and suffering. Let's save our energy to attack the other side instead of unemployed Americans."

Or perhaps we should just laugh along.

After all, all comedy should be allowed. All speech is free. Let's see those conservatives laugh at everyone, not just working class whites who lose their jobs and are homeless, but also at black people with funny names, Jews who are mad about the Iran deal, women who are fat, immigrants who are ugly, and gays who get HIV.

Oh, wait, we can't go there, can we? You see, you can make fun of white Americans who are suffering, jobless, hopeless, and hungry. That's fine. But all of those other jokes would be hate speech.

When you selectively single out my speech for attack, or when you fail to defend the speech of a man like Roosh, you expose yourself as a hypocrite without any moral principles. You have lost the moral high ground. Free speech is all or nothing. You don't get to pick and choose. There is no hate speech. It is all free speech.

Policing the dark side of the New Right is not my responsibility. Nor is it yours. Whatever happened to the common sense saying "the actions of the minority don't represent the majority?" What they do is their business. I have enough battles to fight. I don't need to fight yours too.

Conservatives, you have already failed me and my friends. You not only failed to have our backs, you stabbed us in the back when given a chance.

I'm too busy to go around renouncing people and denouncing people on demand. Don't ask me to do it. If you want to lump me in with people with whom I don't agree or take my silence as tacit assent... whatever. I'm used to having people lie about me.

If you are not my friend, then I am not yours.

But remember, not being my friend does not make you my enemy.

That's a choice you make. Either tell the truth about me or say nothing.

If you want to lie about me, well, perhaps you should ask Sam Biddle how well that worked out for him. Lying about me is a great way to make an enemy of me.

The New Right: The Good

There's a New Right rising. This New Right isn't interested in the cowardly, self-serving opinions of soft-bodied 60-year old cucks who are ashamed of being men and have surrendered their country to SJWs. We're different.

We don't care if you call us mean.

We don't care if you call us racists.

We don't care if you call us misogynists.

We laugh when you call us mentally ill for lifting weights.

We think it's hilarious that you think our attraction to women somehow merits scorn.

We embrace those labels you throw at us, even as we reject your bogus privilege hierarchy.

And do you know why? Because words like "racist" and "misogynist" don't have any serious meaning anymore. Being branded a racist could once destroy your career, but Leftists and cuckservatives have collectively become the boy who cried wolf. I get called a racist and a misogynist every day and it doesn't hurt me in the slightest. Milo Yiannopoulos has become a star *because* he is called a racist and a misogynist every single day.

To paraphrase a classic line from *The Incredibles*, when everybody is racist, when everybody is misogynistic, nobody is. Or at least, nobody cares.

Illegitimate is the New Legitimate

Over the years my rhetoric has become more heated and extreme, and for a good reason.

For years, I primarily wrote about the obvious double standards that applied to men and women. I wrote about my enjoyment of female companionship and I explained the increase in the number of false rape accusations and the growing risk to men of being falsely accused of rape.

Thirty years ago no one would have paid me any attention at all, but that's not because my views are so outlandish and shocking. I'd have simply been too banal to even notice. The times have changed. Today, what should objectively be nothing more than boring and perfectly normal observations about the world classify me as an edgelord.

Defending a man's due process rights in rape trial and campus rape hearings should not be edgy. It should be conventional and safe. It should be respectable. It should be the decent thing to do. Everyone respects the right to due process in literally every other crime in the books, so why should a crime as serious as rape be the exception?

When I defended the concept of due process, I was called "vile" and a "genuine misogynist" by Cathy Young in *Reason* magazine, siding with Matt Binder, an SJW who lied about me. She stated, "Any backlash against radical feminism is likely to serve as a magnet for people who are genuine misogynists, such as pro-GamerGate lawyer Mike Cernovich whose numerous vile tweets were exposed by GamerGate opponent Matt Binder." A number of the Tweets exposing my so-called misogyny were insults I'd hurled *at other men*, which apparently passes as misogyny nowadays.

Note, by the way, that the other libertarian writers at *Reason* have never deemed it worthwhile to disavow or even correct any of the false and unprovoked attacks against me.

These are the very people who don't care when Cathy Young and others like her mock working-class white Americans. But how do they countenance those attacks made by their colleagues while calling me out for mean tweets at the same time. If attacking people is wrong, then why do they not have my back when people attack me unprovoked?

Because, of course, like our conservative friends at *National Review*, the writer at *Reason* who attacked me is more interested in virtue-signaling to SJWs than she is in actually reporting the truth.

That needs to change.

My hope is that our faction of the New Right is one where men are able to unite for common causes and set aside racial and other differences we might have. I have no interest in racism and anti-Semitism. But more importantly, I have no interest in feminism, in equalitarianism, in anti-fascism, or other forms of virtue-signaling and appeasing the Left.

Note: What is racism? Criticizing blacks for acting badly is not racist. Nor is indifference to Israel anti-Semitism. Uniting for political reasons as whites is also not racist, given how every other racial and ethnic group forms caucuses. Hating blacks or Jews or Eskimos for no other reason than their being black, Jewish, or Eskimo is the real issue. Identifying as a white man and defending your own interests is not.

What's really going to happen?

As illegitimate as I am by mainstream standards, my core message is relatively moderate.

I want to be able to run my businesses. I want to be able to sell my books. I want to enjoy sex with women. I want to be able to manage my social media profiles on the same footing as others.

Ever notice that repeated death threats against white men and rape threats against white women are permitted, whereas a single tweet is all it takes for someone like me or Glenn Reynolds to get suspended?

Straight white men should not be accused of committing original sin by being born straight, white, and male. We don't need to confess our sins by checking our privilege.

All straight white men have due process rights. Just like everyone else.

In short, I want equal treatment under the law. That's boring, old-school stuff. Or at least, it should be.

If women can unite for causes common to them, then men can too. And should!

If you're going to allow blacks, Hispanics, Jews, and every other racial group to form political interest groups and factions based on their ethnicity, then you must allow whites to do the same thing. Refusing to allow one specific race to collectively participate in the modern political process is, I daresay, racist.

As a man with a particular disdain for identity politics, I would much rather see all such race-based causes disappear. But that's never going to happen. We are living in a post-ideological age. The rules of the game have changed. We are now living in a world of identity politics.

The White Party, or even the White Male Party, is absolutely appropriate in a time when identity politics are how the game is played.

When a feminist pulls a fire alarm to disrupt a meeting of men discussing men's issues, as happened at the University of Toronto, she should be arrested. Just like a man would be.

When a rabid female SJW physically attacks Roosh, she should be arrested for assault. Just like a man would be.

No one should wonder if Roosh might have had it coming, or deserved to be assaulted, because he wrote books that others do not like. Instead of telling Roosh how he can avoid being attacked by watching his words, we should teach feminists how to behave like decent, law-abiding human beings.

In a time when Roosh and other men regularly face death threats in response to perfectly lawful speech, we need to start spreading the word to garner support for them from men and women around the world. Free speech is in everyone's interest. If they get away with policing Roosh's speech, what makes you think they won't eventually try to police yours?

Either call out the bad behavior by all sides, or silence yourself and call out none of it. Although, I suppose there is always a third option, which is to be a hypocrite. It's up to you. It's your life and your call. But I wouldn't recommend it. You have to live with yourself, after all.

Is equal treatment too much for us to ask?

In the absence of equal treatment for men, and for working-class people, here is what is likely to happen.

- Mainstream pundits will continue to attack men and laugh when they are sent to prison and expelled from colleges after false rape accusations.

- Job losses and homelessness will continue to be funny when they happen to white working class people.

- Male suicide, which is four times the rate of female suicide, will remain a laughing matter.

Let's just highlight one case of mainstream feminist hypocrisy that occurred on the all-female CBS talk show, *The Talk*. The only way I can describe the show is to ask you to picture *The View*, but even less intelligent and insightful, if you can imagine that! The hosts were gleefully discussing a story about a woman who took revenge on her husband who had filed for a divorce by drugging his food, then, as he lay down feeling sick, tied him to the bed and cut off his penis with a kitchen knife before grinding it up in the garbage disposal.

And the response from the sadistic hens of *The Talk*? One host, Sharon Osbourne (yes, Ozzy's wife) declared, "I don't know the circumstances… however, I do think it's fabulous."

Now, imagine the reverse had occurred. What would the response from those women had been if a man had drugged his wife, cut her breasts off, and ground them into hamburger? Would they have been chuckling and declaring his act of spousal mutilation to be "fabulous"?

And while we're speaking of failed marriages, keep in mind the unfortunate man victimized by his ex-wife-to-be is a rarity in more than one way, as 70 percent of divorces are initiated by women. And how do those turn out? Men almost never get custody of their children, and can expect to see their net worth cut in half, regardless of why the divorce took place. The idiots over at *Everyday Feminism* blame these consequences on patriarchal gender norms, because apparently we men are so stupid that we have designed a system that oppresses both women and ourselves.

I suppose you might think men are really that stupid if you watch how men are portrayed in commercials these days.

Nevertheless, all of this is nonsense, and men are beginning to wake up.

Men will increasingly become more militant, and militant men tend to become nationalists.

Sooner or later, the pendulum always swings back, so it may already be too late to stop the angry march of neo-fascism in the United States.

Until then, I'll do my part to keep the peace.

Unfortunately politics is not a hobby for me. It's a way of life, as our very liberty and economic freedom is under attack.

I could be killed for being a white straight man and virtually no one besides those of you reading would care.

National Review wouldn't care. *Reason* magazine wouldn't care. No mainstream writer or publication would care.

They think I deserve to die.

Indeed, they think we all deserve to die.

So it's time for us to look out for one another.

We have enough of our own problems to address, and charity starts at home.

It might seem like you're alone, but you're not.

There are a lot of us, we are here, and we have your back.

It's going to be a long march to freedom, but you already knew it was never going to be easy to be a man.

Stay strong out there.

The War on Masculinity

In a battle between men, the most masculine will win. In a battle between women, the most feminine will win. Understand these two basic laws of nature, and everything from why some men attract more girls than others to the rise of Donald Trump makes complete sense.

What does the War on Men have to do with Donald Trump? More than you'd think.

The War on Men is a war of attrition. Every man is under incessant attack from the moment he is born. Everyone, from school teachers to television shows, from church preachers to media pundits, tells men that we are garbage. We are privileged. We are sinners. We are rapists. We need to be taught not to rape. Resisting all the constant brainwashing takes courage and determination. It takes an act of will.

Even gorillas are under attack. Rest in peace, Harambe.

Even so, if you develop a sense of masculinity, cultivate a dominant mindset, and manage to avoid false rape accusations and divorce courts, then today is the best day in the history of the world to be a man.

As more men become casualties of the war on them, those left standing will reap the spoils of war. The War on Men is creating an aristocracy of masculinity among men.

For a man who grew up in a poor family, or even a middle-class one, the War on Men is an ironic godsend. You can now live a life that was once available only to Roman emperors or billionaires even if you had no head start in life.

Look at my life. I grew up poor and dirty and soft. I'm a dumb hick from flyover country.

By the standards set by mainstream society, I should not have amounted to much.

And yet, I travel the world, I am a legal scholar and a lawyer, and I am a well-known, best-selling author.

There's not a single critic of mine who is more accomplished or lives a better life. They call me an asshole. They call me a narcissist. They call me a jerk. But my credentials stand on their own and aren't subject to attack.

There's no secret to why I'm successful. I embraced my masculinity. I live my life as an unrepentant man who is not ashamed to be a man.

Most men have fallen to the war on masculinity. There are few masculine men remaining in the West.

Take a look around you. The lack of masculine men is astounding!

Most men never touch a barbell. They are dragged around by women, carrying their purses for them. They lack any sense of self-possession, or self-discipline, and often they throw temper tantrums like a child. They appeal to others for sympathy, and to fix their problems for them.

The average man's only respite from an oppressive daily grind is putting on a sports jersey to watch other men perform athletic feats, but even those TV athletes are speech-policed and hen-pecked by the SJWs in ESPN's corporate office.

The GOP is full of demasculinized men. Even worse, the Republican Party establishment is a collection of pedophile-loving cucks.

Look at *National Review*. Is there a single writer for an ostensibly conservative publication whom you'd ask for advice on how to be a man? Is there any big-name, mainstream writer for the Right who looks like he could handle himself in a fight? Maybe Steven Crowder, but he's not a cuckservative.

George Will and his pathetic bow ties are an emblem for the conservative intellectual. Can you imagine him going hunting, or fishing, or even attending a bullfight like Ernest Hemingway?

I previously mentioned the *National Review writer* Charles C.W. Cooke, who is so emasculated that he found himself publicly sympathizing with an admitted pedophile. Cooke was triggered when he saw normal men like me attack *Salon* for publishing an article normalizing pedophilia. Mounting his trusty steed of outrage, Cooke rushed to white-knight in defense of pedophilia.

Salon, an openly pro-pedophile, anti-male publication, and *National Review* are of the same mind.

Why would Cooke ever do that? Because normal male sexuality is masculine, and powerful, and adult, and therefore it is both disgusting and frightening to these feminized, sexually underdeveloped freaks.

Sex with children, which is the result of a weak and deformed mind, is now celebrated by the Left and the Right alike.

These so-called men on the Right do not even have the balls to stand up against pedophiles. How could they possibly stump Trump?

Donald Trump's rise in the polls came as a surprise to nearly everyone but me. People seriously thought I was crazy when I said Trump would win the general election, and most were certain he'd fade away quickly in the early Republican primaries.

Nearly two years ago, I noted that I could put a Republican into the Oval Office. People laughed, as they often do, as they do not understand the War on Men.

I tweeted: "I'm a libertarian, so I don't care much about elections. But I could put a Republican into the Oval Office thanks to the SJWs."

I was speaking about my ideology, of course, not me personally. And I was right, as Donald Trump's rise has shown. In a contest between men, the most masculine will win.

Trump is winning because he's masculine. The only way to stump Trump is to out-man him.

Was there a single masculine candidate other than Donald Trump? Ted Cruz is a a little bit of a man's man, although Cruz is flabby and has an unfortunate, soft-looking, fish face. The man also needs to start lifting weights.

Jeb Bush was a low-energy dope. Trump branding him that was all it took to knock him out of the race. As Mark Steyn perfectly phrased it, Trump took down a $100 million candidate with an *adjective*.

Jeb stumbled over himself every time he tried to respond to Trump's attacks, looking like a deer caught in the headlights all the while. Bush's value as a man is shown by his mate selection. A masculine man always dates up. The son of the 41st President of the United States didn't exactly do that. I'll leave it at that.

Rand Paul is a curly-haired trust fund kid riding daddy's coattails. When Randie got on his knees before Al Sharpton, he was done.

And Marco? Little Marco? Enough said.

Donald Trump has embraced his masculinity and his success.

What's not to like about Trump? He has it all. He is more productive at 70 than most of us will ever be in our primes.

He's rich.

He has total personal freedom.

His wife is gorgeous.

He has a large family, and his children have not only avoided the usual celebrity scandals, but they actually like him and want to help him.

No other candidate is man enough to take him out.

What can you learn from Trump?

Stop being so apologetic. Stand up for yourself. Go pick a fight if one doesn't find you.

Work harder. A man should work 12-hour days. If you don't want to work long hours, it's because you're not living your passion.

If you're not, then find your passion. If you can't afford to work your passion full time, spend one hour each day working on your passion. Eventually you'll be able to work on it full time.

Date women who are more beautiful than you are handsome. Normal men date at their level. Weak men date down. Strong men date up.

It takes incredible self-confidence to date a woman who you know has numerous options. When you're strong enough to let a beautiful woman walk out the door without begging her to stay or chasing after her, you've made it as a man.

Leave a legacy. Write a book like *Gorilla Mindset* or *The Art of the Deal*, build massive buildings, or create a business your children can run after you're gone.

If you're a father, put down your smartphone and spend time with your children. One might well say the only way to judge a man is to look at his children. They are, after all, your most important legacy.

And most of all, never, never, *never* apologize for being a man.

Scott Adams and the Master Persuader Hypothesis

No book on Trump's rise would be complete without a look at Scott Adams. While he became famous for creating the comic strip Dilbert, Adams is also a powerful writer on mindset and persuasion. His semi-autobiographical book, *How to Fail at Nearly Everything Yet Still Win at Life,* is one of the best books ever written on how to live a life of power and inspiration.

As a trained hypnotist and masterful marketer, Adams was also able to predict Trump's rise even though all the statisticians couldn't create a model that accurately predicted Trump as the eventual nominee. Back in August 2015, Adams said that Trump would win the presidency in a landslide. He was called a fool by the chattering class. Adam's prediction even preceded my own, depending on how you define a prediction. While I rightly called Trump's rise, Adams made a concrete and falsifiable prediction.

According to Adams, Trump's rise is explained less by underlying cultural forces and more by Trump himself. Trump's success in the polls stems from his sheer force of character combined with our human nature as flawed thinkers. To understand Adams, you must understand his Master Persuader hypothesis, as well as his Moist Robot theory.

In Adams's view, human beings are not rational. To paraphrase Winston Churchill, a brief conversation with the average voter will confirm this. Instead of being rational, our minds are malleable, and thus susceptible to manipulation. We can be reprogrammed by ourselves, or, if we aren't careful, by others.

Adams's Moist Robot theory is not mere speculation, as extensive research into cognitive biases has reliably shown that the brain tends to take mental shortcuts. Our brains like to do the least amount of work possible. These shortcuts our brains take often work to our detriment, and it takes training to avoid falling into thought traps. Perhaps the worst kind of shortcut is one the partisan mind takes when it filters out all information from the opposing side and categorizes it as untrustworthy.

The Master Persuader hypothesis posits that there are skilled communicators who can persuade us of almost anything. And, as you can probably guess, Donald Trump is one of those master persuaders, according to Scott Adams.

Adams argues that Trump's policy decisions do not account for his political rise. Instead, Adams observes that Trump is one of the most persuasive people to have ever walked the earth. Adams notes that Trump often A/B tests his message—Trump tries out two different variants to see which one works better—and is always willing to accept criticism for walking back his statements if they meet with an excessively negative response. For example, early in his campaign, Trump suggested that the U.S. should take in Syrian refugees. After Trump read my original reporting from Europe on the matter, which explained that most of these refugees were men of prime-fighting age, Trump immediately changed his position. The risk of importing ISIS is too dangerous, Trump said, after reading my reports. But this is not simple flip-flopping, as it is sometimes wrongly characterized. It's adapting to a deeper understanding of the situation.

However, if Trump were relying solely on his status as a master persuader to win the election, he'd never need to walk back any controversial policy statements or adapt his positions. He'd simply move past them using the raw force of his persuasive power.

That is not what Trump does, though. As the *Washington Post* reported, Trump publicly A/B tests his message in speeches. If a joke doesn't land, or a policy position doesn't change any minds or attract sufficient attention, Trump immediately moves on from the dud. Trump has also made immigration policy the center of his campaign for President. Immigration is a massively important issue to the majority of Americans. When Congress repeatedly tried enacting immigration amnesty, in 2005, 2006, 2009, 2013, and 2014, Americans revolted each and every time.

You may recall that Marco Rubio briefly appeared to be the favorite to win the Republican nomination in 2016. But as a member of the infamous Gang of 8, his support for immigration amnesty and his unwillingness to increase border security destroyed his chance of winning the Republican primaries.

Trump also relies heavily on nationalism and identity-based rhetoric in his campaign. Trump is running a campaign to restore the American identity. Trump wouldn't need to tap into nationalist or populist ideals if his persuasive abilities alone were enough to win him the presidency.

Now Adams is perfectly aware that all master persuaders change their positions from time to time. But changing your message based on audience feedback or data-testing proves that talking points matter. Trump would not have any chance to win the election if he had run as a Democrat promising to bring socialism to the United States. Or, for that matter, as a Republican doing the same.

In an interview during which we discussed Donald Trump, Scott told me this. "My take is that Trump, as a persuader, knows how to choose emotionally powerful topics. So the issues DO matter, but there is a reason he chose the issues he picked, and a reason no one else with fairly similar policies, such as Ted Cruz, succeeded. Picking your battles is part of persuasion in my expansive definition. Could Trump have won with Bernie's policies? In my opinion, yes. But he would have changed it from 'Just gimme free stuff' to something more persuasive."

But whether it is his master persuader abilities or his chosen policies, Donald Trump has combined a message of nationalism with powerful persuasive skills and unapologetic masculinity. And in the end, that is what is fueling his rise to Make America Great Again.

Part 2: Media

In the future, Donald Trump's treatment of the media as well as the way he uses social media will be studied by everyone from marketers to political operatives running campaigns. More than any candidate who ever ran for office before, Trump has been able to "Trump the media" by keeping these two maxims in mind: Conflict is Attention and Attention is Influence.

It requires a deep familiarity with the power of the mass media to fully appreciate the impossible odds Trump has faced during his presidential campaign. He has been attacked by everyone from fraudulent newspaper pundits to the hoax-happy television media. And in order to understand how stacked the odds were against him, and how Trump has forced the media to tell the truth against its will, it is necessary to first take a look at just how bad, and how corrupt, the opinion-makers and journalists are.

The way the media programs the public, the way its opinion-makers make your opinions, is through programming your mindset. Mindset, which you'll learn a lot more about in the next section, controls every area of your life.

> *A mindset is a set of assumptions, methods, or notations held by one or more people or groups of people that is so established that it creates a powerful incentive within these*

people or groups to continue to adopt or accept prior be-
haviors, choices, or tools.

—"Mindset", from *Infogalactic*, the planetary
knowledge core

Consider your basic assumptions about the media. Do you believe the media has moral authority? Do you believe the media is
honest? Is the U.S. media "the free press" and "the Fourth Estate"?
Is the "free press" independent and treated with respect by the establishment or is it a tool to be manipulated and used?

The answers to those questions today will be very different than
they would have been decades ago. Americans once held the press
in great esteem and we were proud of our free press, which stood in
stark contradiction to the government-controlled presses in Com-
munist China and Soviet Russia. Journalists were respected tellers
of uncomfortable truths who "comforted the afflicted and afflicted
the comfortable." When serious news anchors like Walter Cronkite
spoke, everyone listened.

When you respect the press, your mindset is one of deference.
You believe what you read. You believe what you are told.

But Donald Trump knew that by 2016, things had completely
changed. He knew that the press had been a scam living off its
past reputation for decades. The American media was now among
the least trustworthy in the world, as its institutions had named
Hitler the man of the year, praised Joseph Stalin, denied the Soviet
atrocities in the Ukraine, and even warned of a coming Ice Age.

Trump began to develop his formidable skill at trolling the media when, as a prominent Manhattan real estate developer, he found
himself facing relentless attacks from the *New York Times*. Because
so many state and local officials held the *Times* in high regard, a negative review from an architectural columnist could sideline a project
for years. In *The Art of the Deal*, Trump wrote: "It irritates me that

critics, who've neither designed nor built anything themselves, are given carte blanche to express their views in the pages of major publications, whereas the targets of their criticism are almost never offered space to respond."

Trump initially fought back against the media by writing scathing open letters to the press, holding press conferences, and even pretending to be his own publicist in order to feed stories to hungry gossip newsmongers.

When the media publicly shames a target, the individuals targeted often feel hurt. But feeling hurt by negative press coverage is simply a reflection of your mindset. Why should you care if people who are known scoundrels, sociopaths, and even *pedophiles* attack you in public, when their hatred and opposition is a positive testimony of your character?

Trump learned to reject the moral legitimacy of the press early in his career. His media mindset developed, as he decided that he was going to play the press rather than let the press play him.

Imagine having a job where you could say whatever you wanted, be wrong 99 percent of the time, say terrible things about everyone you hate, and still keep your job. Now imagine that the more obnoxious and nasty you are, the higher you will be promoted. If that sounds too good to be true, then you should really meet the professional pundit class. They are bigger prostitutes than the average crack whore.

Many people believe that pundits and commentators are paid directly for their commentary. Although most people who appear on TV or write for mainstream publications do indeed draw a modest salary or get paid as little as $15 for an article or an appearance, the true source of the elite pundit's income is undisclosed payments by various business oligarchs and sugar daddies. Pundits aren't paid to tell the truth and they aren't paid to share their honest observations of the world. They are paid for pretending to be journalists or public commentators while agitating for causes their paymasters support.

Did you know, for example, that the *New York Times* is owned by Carlos Slim, a Mexican billionaire who earns his living by running a series of monopolies. Slim profits from illegal immigration in several ways, the most important through the profits he earns by owning all of the phone lines in Mexico.

Journalist Larry Luxner reported in 2002: "In August 1998, Telmex launched 'Mexico En Linea'—a program that allows expatriate Mexicans living in the United States to purchase phone lines for family and friends back home…. Telmex USA has received around one million applications for phone lines, of which 70 percent are generally approved."

Now ask yourself this question. Why would an incredibly successful businessman like Slim invest in the *New York Times*, a failing business in a rapidly shrinking industry? The *Times*, as recent tax returns revealed, has been run at a loss for years. It's obvious that Slim isn't going to make any money from it. So, has he lost his touch? Or does he have other, more devious reasons for wanting to own it? Because while Slim loses money directly through his investment in the *New York Times*, what he buys with those losses is an army of highly-regarded political bloggers who are willing to unhesitatingly lie about Donald Trump on his behalf.

Will it surprise you to know that the *New York Times* stopped covering Slim's monopolistic practices after he made his investment in it? It shouldn't. While the media huffs and puffs about Russia's nonexistent influence over the U.S. media, no one seems to dare ask the obvious question: Does Mexico control the *New York Times*?

Now you should understand why Amazon founder Jeff Bezos bought the *Washington Post*. He didn't buy it to make money off it, he bought it to influence you.

Now perhaps, like a lot of conservatives, you think that the left-wing pundits may be owned by the Left, but the right-wing pundits of the conservative media are fighting hard for the American people. If so, I'm afraid I'll have to disappoint you. Fox News proudly calls Douglas E. Schoen a contributor. Who is Douglas E. Schoen? Schoen is a former Clinton family operative, which is bad enough in itself. It gets worse.

Believe it or not, Schoen's primary financial benefactor appears to be a billionaire Ukranian oligarch who wants the United States to go to war with Russia.

In a remarkable conflict-of-interest, Fox News analyst and former Clinton operative Douglas E. Schoen failed to disclosed to readers that he was paid millions of dollars by Ukrainian agents, presumably in order to incite a war between the United States and Russia. Before being hired by the Ukrainians, Schoen worked for Bill Clinton and earned $40,000 a month brokering meetings between then-Secretary of State Hillary Clinton and various billionaire oligarchs. Schoen has more than 30 years experience as a pollster and political consultant. In addition to being a Fox News analyst, he is the co-host of "Fox News Insiders" which is televised on Sundays on the Fox News Channel at 7 pm EST.

In the lead-up to the 2016 election, it been reported that Schoen has been paid *millions* of dollars by Victor Pinchuk, Ukranian oligarch, a former member of Ukrainian parliament, and a confederate of George Soros.

Pinchuk was a member of Ukrainian parliament from 1998 to 2006, which means that Schoen was being paid $40,000 a month by a representative of a foreign government while maintaining close ties to both the former President and the current Secretary of State. Schoen started as an errand boy for Pinchuk, using his access to the Clinton family to arrange meetings in much the same manner he had before. *Russia Today* reported that "from 2009 up to 2013, the year the Ukrainian crisis erupted, the Clinton Foundation received at least $8.6 million from the Victor Pinchuk Foundation."

But why was Pinchuk paying Schoen all that money? We can't know for certain, but based on Schoen's appearances on Fox News, it appears that Schoen has moved well beyond conventional Clinton-style grab-the-cash corruption and into professional cheerleading for a war between the United States and Russia. Americans who lobby for foreign governments are required to register as Foreign Agents under the Foreign Agents Registration Act. The Department of Justice makes these reports, along with financial disclosures, available to the public, which is why we know about Schoen's compensation and who is paying him. And yet, incredibly, Fox News *does not require its analysts to disclose these ties*. Schoen's biography is for all to see on Fox News. Look it up. Notice what is missing. His real job, and his ties to Pinchuk, go completely unmentioned.

Schoen regularly writes about the Ukraine at FoxNews.com. In one article called "In a world of chaos, the only clear winner is Vladimir Putin," Schoen wrote:

> *Before Putin illegally annexed Crimea, Clinton went to Yalta and warned the Russians against aggression. The Russians came anyway. Since then, she has scarcely criticized the administration for its refusal to meaningfully aid an increasingly desparate Ukraine.... Putin has a clear strategy that has propelled him to military victory in Crimea, and he holds strong positions in Syria and Ukraine. He is on a mission to advance Russian inter-*

ests around the world and reestablish Russia as a global
superpower. We are doing nothing to stop him, and our
politicians have no serious plan for the future.

Schoen doesn't only write about Vladimir Putin, of course. With the election approaching, he also wrote about the two presidential candidates and their positions on foreign policy. Specifically, their foreign policies concerning Russia and Ukraine, in an article co-authored with Judith Miller entitled "On foreign policy, Hillary Clinton leans more to the Right than Donald Trump."

On Russia, while Mrs. Clinton has called Putin a "bully"
and has described the relationship between Washington
and Moscow as "complicated," Mr. Trump has floated the
idea of establishing a new alliance with Russia, whose co-
operation he says is needed to help end the six-year war
in Syria, fight terrorism, and diffuse tensions. While he
says that more should be done to support Ukraine, which
has been battling Russia-backed separatists since Russia
annexed Crimea, he has not detailed what specifically he
would do to help end Russia's occupation of Crimea and
combat Russian meddling in Kiev's internal affairs.

Schoen's biography appears at the bottom of these anti-Russian, pro-Ukraine articles. But nowhere does he mention his handsome yearly stipend or the millions of dollars he was paid by a member of the Ukrainian parliament.

Foreign money controls U.S. media. Even Fox News is on the take. And until Fox News and all the other media outlets require their guests to disclose these gargantuan financial conflicts of interest, you must assume everything you read or hear was bought and paid for. The mainstream media is, for all practical purposes, dead.

There are almost no real journalists left anymore. Even the contrib-
utors at "conservative" Fox News are nothing more than the paid
mouthpieces of oligarchs and billionaires.

For decades, traditional conservatives complained about the
"liberal mainstream media." This proved to be completely ineffec-
tive. Even though only 6 percent of the public trusts the media,
according to Gallup, until the 2016 election, each and every political candidate needed the media in order to get his message out
to the public. The 2012 Republican nominee, Mitt Romney often
complained, legitimately, about the bias of the liberal media against
him while trying to get press coverage from the very people he was
complaining about. He didn't have a choice, because without press
coverage, no candidacy had any chance for success.

Despite nominally conservative media outlets like Fox News
and the *Wall Street Journal*, there was no way for a Republican to
get his message directly out to the people without going through
the filter of the mainstream media. That began to change some-
time between 2011 and 2013, a process which accelerated greatly
in 2015.

Donald Trump joined Twitter in March 2009. He became an
active user of social media. Whereas most people view social media
as a way to keep up with friends and share cat pics, Trump saw
an opportunity to create his own media empire using, as real estate
investors are often fond of saying, other people's money. Or in this
case, other people's technology. Trump was an early, and active,
Twitter user.

"Twitter is like owning the *New York Times* without the losses,"
Trump once explained when asked why he makes such active use of
the platform. "Before if you wanted to get your message out, you
had to call a press conference. Now you can post it onto Twitter

and it reaches the people directly."

Trump has 12.5 million followers. The *New York Times* has a daily print circulation of 590,000. Trump doesn't need the *New York Times*. In fact, the *New York Times* needs him!

Through the use of social media, Trump is able to drive media cycles, draw attention by creating conflict, and bust hoaxes the same day they appear. As you'll see from my case studies, I have used social media in a similar manner; although I only have 133,000 followers, my own Twitter account received over 115 million impressions in September 2016. Imagine how many impressions Trump's 12.5 million followers must produce! I have also created news cycles by utilizing the same technique of bypassing the crooked and dishonest gatekeepers of the mainstream media.

Before we go into how Trump plays the media, and show how you can do it too, let me show you first that the media is *entirely* dishonest. This is important, because, as it is said, you can't con an honest man.

Now, you might think that the media's bias and dishonesty is overstated by Trump and others like me. Although, given that only six percent of the general public trust the media, you'd think multinational corporations like the *New York Times* and *Washington Post* would treat public perception of their dishonesty as a serious brand crisis. But they haven't shown much concern about this, as even their half-hearted efforts at launching so-called fact-checking sites has done nothing to redeem their brands. 71 percent of voters distrust those fact-checking websites, too, and for good reason. Every mainstream media outlet has repeatedly revealed its bias in various ways, even to the point of trying to sell the public on outright hoaxes.

Let's have a look at media bias first, before we get into the more extreme examples.

Hillary Clinton's refusal to give a press conference, and the subsequent media cover-up.

Hillary Clinton went over 275 days without giving a press conference. This is a modern record for a presidential candidate. While Hillary refused to give a single press conference to her media allies, Trump appeared in front of the press regularly. He showed up on nearly every possible television outlet, gave speeches around the country, and held multiple press conferences too.

Recognizing the media had no intention of holding Clinton accountable for avoiding them, I created an online viral campaign using Twitter to trend a hashtag. We mocked Clinton as "#HidingHillary," and started another hashtag called #WheresHillary, which actually trended number one in the world. Trump himself tweeted it. At my suggestion, one reader created a clock counting the days, hours, and minutes since Clinton's last press conference.

Jeff Bezos's personal bloggers at "The Fix", a *Washington Post* politics site, finally noticed how interested people were in this. They began to copy me, and they created their own clock without crediting me with the idea. It only took 250 days for them to write about Clinton's refusal to hold a press conference.

25 days later, a full 275 days after Hillary Clinton's previous press conference, Brian Stelter finally broke the TV news blackout on the subject of CNN.

When Trump went 55 days without giving a press conference, it was headline news on CNN, even though he gave SIXTEEN press conferences during Hillary's long public silence. And Hillary Clinton went five times as long without giving a press conference before the media made an issue of it.

Bias can be difficult to prove. Clearly, however, there is a demonstrable double standard at work here. There is no way to justify or rationalize the different treatment the two candidates received other than media bias.

John McCain's health vs Hillary Clinton's health.

Another clear example of media bias is the different ways in which the media treated the health issues of John McCain and Hillary Clinton. In 2008, the media made a major issue out of McCain's health. After being bombarded by media demands to see his medical records, McCain finally gave in and turned them over to the media.

Eight years later, the media shamelessly stated that Hillary Clinton's health was off limits. When I and others began raising the issue, the *Washington Post* devoted several stories seeking to discredit us. Despite a lengthy history of health problems that included multiple falls, concussions, and seizures, any questions about Clinton's health were dismissed as conspiracy theory.

On September 11, 2016, Clinton had a seizure while being escorted to her car during a memorial event. She collapsed, and appeared to have completely lost consciousness. If this event had not been caught on camera by an interested citizen who happened to be filming, there is absolutely no question that the media would have covered it up.

Hillary Clinton clearly has severe health problems. It is obvious to even the most casual observer. But whereas the media insisted McCain prove what turned out to be his good health, they decided that the public should not be allowed to know anything

about Hillary Clinton's health. The double standard is unjustifi-
able. The bias is undeniable.

The media refuses to cover violence against Trump sup-
porters.

Another startling example of media bias is the way in which the
media refuses to cover even the most sensational violence against
Donald Trump's supporters. Trump supporters have found their car
vandalized by Clinton supporters merely because they had a bumper
sticker on it. Scott Adams famously endorsed Hillary Clinton for his
own protection, because being a Trump supporter in liberal North-
ern California was a threat to his safety. A Wisconsin woman was
arrested for disorderly conduct after smearing peanut butter on 30
cars belonging to members of a local conservation group because she
thought they were Trump supporters.

If this is the first time you've heard of these stories, you're not
alone. Only those who follow my Twitter account on a regular basis are aware of many of these attacks on Trump supporters, as the
mainstream media covers them up.

The attacks reached a fevered pitch in San Jose, California.
Trump supporters were run down and beaten by mobs of left-wing
thugs. One woman had eggs thrown on her and was openly men-
aced by a crowd of men. Neither feminists nor liberal journalists
like CNN's Anderson Cooper bothered to cover those stories.

Chicago was even worse. Trump had to cancel a rally due to
riots protesting his visit there. And a Republican office in North
Carolina was destroyed with a fire-bomb; fortunately no one was
inside it.

When fights break out at Trump rallies, it's big news. When Clinton supporters start riots and attack Trump supporters, the media goes silent.

CNN gives air time to a would-be Trump assassin.

During a Trump rally in Dayton, Ohio, Thomas Dimassimo jumped over the rails. He stormed the stage. Never afraid to confront danger, Trump moved toward Dimassimo, although Secret Service agents intervened first. Suspecting that there was more to it than the mainstream media was willing to say, I investigated and uncovered that this was actually a genuine assassination attempt aimed at Trump. Although Dimassimo was only charged with disorderly conduct and inducing panic, he was armed with a knife and a Secret Service agent was wounded in the hand by it.

CNN's response to all of this? They invited Dimassimo to come on air as a guest and treated him as a hero of the social justice movement.

Do you believe for a second that anyone who rushed a stage on which Hillary Clinton was standing, and did it *armed with a knife*, would be given a similar media platform? Of course not!

The major newspaper endorsements.

If you're still not convinced that the media is hopelessly biased, consider this summary of the 2016 presidential endorsements by the major newspapers from Infogalactic.

> *As of October 16, 51 of the nation's 100 largest newspapers by paid circulation have made endorsements. Of these, 43 have endorsed Democratic candidate Hillary Clinton, three endorsed Libertarian candidate Gary Johnson, four gave no endorsement, and USA Today, "in a*

break with more than three decades of precedent, weighed in specifically against [Donald] Trump." Republican candidate Donald Trump has received only two endorsements from daily newspapers thus far, the Santa Barbara News-Press and the St. Joseph News-Press. Such a shunning of a major-party candidate is unprecedented in American history.

The double standards are clear. When a Republican is running for office, nothing is off limits. When a Democrat is running for office, there are special rules that apply, depending upon the candidate. Trump has had to break these rules, as the mainstream media has gone from merely tilting the balance against the Republican candidate to openly stacking the deck against him.

As if media bias weren't bad enough, the media has been caught hoaxing the public dozens of times in recent year. There have been over 100 known hate crime hoaxes spread by the media. We all heard about the rape hoaxes at Duke University, and no one can forget the infamous Rolling Stone rape hoax. However two anti-Trump media hoaxes from 2016 stand out in particular.

The Michelle Fields hoax.

Michelle Fields, like many privileged people who never had to work for a living, was desperate for fame. Unable to achieve it through her reporting, she decided to make what she thought would be a surefire move to get it. She falsely accused Trump's campaign manager of assaulting her. The Michelle Fields hoax spread like wildfire through both the conservative and mainstream medias, proving that few people on either the Right or Left are at all interested in the truth.

Fields's then-boyfriend, now fiancé, Jamie Weinstein, a senior editor at *The Daily Caller* posted on Twitter, "Trump always surrounds himself w thugs. Tonight thug Corey Lewandowski tried to pull my gf @MichelleFields to the ground when she asked tough q."

That tweet was heard round the world, and soon Fields's story was written up in the *Washington Post*.

In an article titled, "Inside Trump's inner circle, his staffers are willing to fight for him. Literally," a *Washington Post* blogger wrote that Trump's campaign manager Lewandowski violently grabbed Michelle Fields and nearly threw her to the ground. The story revealed a frightening tale of drama: "Fields stumbled. Finger-shaped bruises formed on her arm. 'I'm just a little spooked,' she said, a tear streaming down her face."

According to her official statement, an article entitled, "Michelle Fields: In Her Own Words," the following happened that fateful night: "I was jolted backwards. Someone had grabbed me tightly by the arm and yanked me down. I almost fell to the ground, but was able to maintain my balance. Nonetheless, I was shaken."

Fields's wounded bird story produced the fifteen minutes of fame she was seeking. Fields became a daily presence on CNN and MSNBC, and she even appeared on Megan Kelly's show on Fox News.

There was just one problem. The whole story was a hoax.

Video later surfaced that showed Lewandowski walking by Fields. She was not not grabbed. She was not nearly thrown to the ground. She showed absolutely no sign of physical or mental distress when Lewandowski happened to brush past her.

Yet Fields insisted she was a victim. Everyone from so-called conservatives like Ben Shapiro to radical feminists insisted Fields had been badly wronged.

Lloyd Grove of *The Daily Beast* wrote an article supporting the Fields-as-victim narrative. In his article, Grove made up a conversation. Supposedly, hours after the incident, Lewandowski told Breitbart's Washington, D.C. editor, Matthew Boyle, that he manhandled Fields, according to an unnamed, and, as it turned out, nonexistent source.

The Michelle Fields hoax wasn't just a case of media bias. Michelle Fields did not have a tear running down her eye. She did not almost fall to the ground. She was not assaulted. The media instead created a hoax in order to try to harm Trump's presidential campaign.

The Trump "debases" women hoax.

Not to be outdone by the *Washington Post*, the *New York Times* created another Donald Trump hoax. Apparently the Grey Lady, as the newspaper is called, has been hoaxing the public a lot longer, because they put a more professional effort into it.

Megan Twohey of the *New York Times* is a master class in how to spot a liar. Twohey along with fellow journalist Michael Barbaro published a hit on Donald Trump called "Crossing the Line: How Donald Trump Behaved with Women in Public." Twohey and Barbaro accused Donald Trump of offensive conduct varying from sexual harassment to "debasing" women. The problem? The story was a hoax, according to one of the very women interviewed for the story.

In her article, Twohey tells the story of Trump ex-girlfriend Rowanne Brewer Lane. Ms. Lane attended a pool party at Trump's property Mar-A-Largo.

"There were about 50 models and 30 men. There were girls in the pools, splashing around. For some reason Donald seemed a little smitten with me. He just started talking to me and nobody else. He suddenly took me by the hand, and he started to show me around the mansion. He asked me if I had a swimsuit with me. I said no. I hadn't intended to swim. He took me into a room and opened drawers and asked me to put on a swimsuit.

"Ms. Brewer Lane, at the time a 26-year-old model, did as Mr. Trump asked. 'I went into the bathroom and tried one on,' she recalled. It was a bikini. 'I came out, and he said, 'Wow.' "

Twohey described this as "a debasing face-to-face encounter between Mr. Trump and a young woman he hardly knew." Never mind that they ended up dating.

Ms. Brewer Lane was outraged that Twohey lied about her, and went public with her own version of events.

"Actually, it was very upsetting. I was not happy to read it at all. Well, because the *New York Times* told us several times that they would make sure that my story that I was telling came across. They promised several times that they would do it accurately. They told me several times and my manager several times that it would not be a hit piece and that my story would come across the way that I was telling it and honestly, and it absolutely was not. They spun it to where it appeared negative. I did not have a negative experience with Donald Trump, and I don't appreciate them making it look like that I was saying that it was a negative experience because it was not."

In a rare moment of honest journalism, an anchor on CNN asked Twohey about her invented story.

> *CNN: You did use the word debase in the piece. Is that a word that Rowanne used used or that the women you spoke to used?*

> *Twohey: So we heard a variety of... I mean... the...*

> *the… descriptions of Rowanne was one of many voices.…*
> *We really value the fact that… and I think that one of the*
> *things you'll see is that…*

In other words, Brewer Lane never used the word "debasing" and she did not view Trump's treatment of her or other women as a problem. There was no story.

As you can see, the media is not only biased, it openly fabricates stories in order to help its favored candidates and harm the candidates it wants to lose.

Fighting the Last War

A military maxim states that today's generals have a bad habit of trying to fight the next war using the outdated methods of the last one. That's exactly what every other GOP candidate has done. No other GOP candidate, except Donald Trump, fought today's media warfare using the tools that are now available to him.

In 2008 and 2012, a candidate who wanted to get his message out to the people had to go through the media gatekeepers. He'd pitch a story idea to reporters and hope they decided to cover it. Or he'd hold a press conference, hoping the media would attend, and hoping the media wouldn't misrepresent what he said too much.

As you've seen from the earlier section, this old model worked amazingly well for the media. It didn't work out so well for the candidates, though. When all the information and messages must be filtered through people who are biased and willing to take sides and lie about what they are transmitting, the media can usually control how the candidates are viewed by the public, and therefore who wins the election.

Voters believe they decide who wins the election. But where do voters get the information that is the basis for their decisions?

When the media controls what information flows to voters, then democracy is a myth. We live in a medioacracy, not a democracy. Trump, however, restored democracy by disrupting the old media model through his adept use of social media.

Trump is able to create news cycles by starting feuds with pubic figures like Megyn Kelly and by hinting that he would not attend a GOP presidential debate, a hint that foreshadowed his subsequent absence, which was a direct warning to the media that they would not be able to control him the way they had controlled his predecessors.

Social media as media.

Social media allowed Trump to create news and dominate the news cycle in two important ways. First, through his millions of readers on Facebook, Twitter, and YouTube, Trump was able to bypass the gatekeepers. Twitter became his 140-character press conference. Trump's love of Twitter ran so deep that at one point, his advisers worried he'd announce his vice presidential pick over Twitter instead of through more appropriate and traditional channels.

When the media hoaxers lied about Trump, he responded quickly by holding a virtual press conference on Twitter. Trump's tweets rapidly went viral, being spread by his millions of followers. Using the ration based on my own impressions, Trump's Twitter is probably doing well over 2 *billion* impressions a month. If that sounds like an exaggerated estimate, consider that my account gets 115 million monthly impressions and Milo Yiannopoulos was running over 200 million before he was banned from Twitter.

Social media allows you to reach your supporters directly, and the mainstream media is terrified by this. Through the power of social media, alternative media personalities like me and Stefan Molyneux of FreeDomainRadio have been able to create news cycles without being dependent in any way upon the mainstream media.

How social media creates news cycles.

A "news cycle" is defined as the media reporting on some event, followed by the media reporting on the reactions of the public to the earlier reports. Re-read that definition. It's important to understand the process. A news cycle traditionally began with the media reporting on some event. Then the public would react to those reports. Then the media would report on the public's reaction. Rinse and repeat. Today, however, the methods have changed. The public is now reacting *to events that are not reported by the media*. And yet, the media is forced to report on the public's reaction to those events. The public, and therefore the media, are reacting to our reports. They are reacting to *us*.

Consider some high-profile examples involving politically incorrect topics.

If you followed the media closely in 2015, you would have believed that there was a refugee crisis involving Syria, and that Syrian refugees are mostly women and children. This narrative was forced down the eyeballs of America readers and viewers. This narrative was also a hoax.

Suspecting that the media was lying, I went to the Keleti train station in Budapest, Hungary, which at the time was a hotspot of the refugee crisis. Through Facebook and Twitter, I reported the truth. Over 70 percent of the "Syrian refugees" were not from Syria, and very few of them were women and children. I saw it with my own eyes, and recorded it with my video camera. They were almost all men of prime fighting age. They were not refugees, but economic migrants. And worse, more than a few of the actual Syrians were ISIS soldiers who have invaded the West under the cover of the refugee crisis as terrorist Trojan horses.

A few months later, in November 2015, one of those poor Syrian war refugees helped murder 120 people in Paris in the Bataclan night club massacre.

Far from being alone, I have been joined by citizen journalists across the world who drive daily news cycles by forcing the media to respond to other stories they would rather bury. For example, the media had been covering up the crimes committed by roving sex gangs of refugees and other immigrants until users on Reddit and other social media platforms exposed the truth.

Journalists have long known that migrants tend to rove in rape gangs. For years, they have had the power to keep this information from the public. But social media has taken away the media's power to silence the real news. Because of citizen journalists, because of people like you reading this book, the mainstream media has been compelled to report on rapefugee activity throughout Europe. The wall of silence has been broken.

Social media has taken away the mainstream media's traditional power to dictate the news cycle and even to decide for voters who will be President. Trump mastered social media and broke the power of the mainstream media over him. But how was he able to do that? What gave Donald Trump the strength and the courage to withstand a furious, non-stop media assault on him, of a duration and an intensity that very few men in history have ever endured?

For that, we need to go deeper. Media influences culture, but as we've seen in this section, one man can influence the media. And that leads us to the question that is the core of this book, what is it that influences that one man?

Part 3: Mindset

Your belief generates the power, the skill, the energy to succeed at achieving your goals.

—Donald Trump

Remember, mindset is "a set of assumptions, methods, or notations held by one or more people or groups of people that is so established that it creates a powerful incentive within these people or groups to continue to adopt or accept prior behaviors, choices, or tools."

As one of the world's few experts on mindset, I recognized Trump's behavior during the Republican primaries was not random, as many pundits had erroneously claimed, but in fact was based on a deep background in mindset. Later evidence confirmed that this was the case, as during a campaign speech in Iowa, Trump mentioned that he had studied under, and attended church with, Norman Vincent Peale, the ground-breaking author of *The Power of Positive Thinking*.

Trump's mindset training began at an early age, as he grew up in the Presbyterian Church during the positive thinking movement led by Peale. In a speech during the Iowa primary campaign, Trump told the audience: "I went to Sunday school. Dr. Norman Vincent Peale, *The Power of Positive Thinking*, was my pastor. To this day one of the great speakers I've seen. You hated to leave church. You hated when the sermon was over. That's how great he was at Marble Collegiate Church."

Gwenda Blair discovered that Trump's parents, Fred and Mary, felt an immediate affinity for Peale's teachings. On Sundays, they drove into Manhattan to worship at Marble Collegiate Church, where Peale was the head pastor. Donald and both his sisters were married there, and funeral services for both Fred and Mary were held there in the main sanctuary."

The Power of Positive Thinking by Norman Vincent Peale, which is reported to have sold as many as 10 million copies, started a nationwide movement. As a result of reading Peale's book, millions of people stopped viewing the world in a negative manner and from a position of scarcity. They learned instead to recognize that today is the greatest time in the history of the world to be alive.

In *The Power of Positive Thinking*, Peale taught that the biggest cause of unhappiness was an individual's own self-doubt and worry. Peale showed people how to stop beating themselves up with negative words and self-destructive thought patterns. He taught his students to think of themselves as great.

Peale's message of positive thinking took root in Trump, who has not only spread Peale's message, but lived it himself.

In an interview from years ago that has since gone viral, with tens of millions of views, a woman asked Trump what average people can do to succeed.

> **Woman from the audience**: *How do I, as an average person, begin?*

> **Trump**: *First of all, never think of yourself as average. You started off with the wrong question. Because you're not average. You have a lot going.... You just have to get that word average out of your vocabulary. You have to tell*

yourself that you're great, and you have to believe it. If you can say it and don't believe it, it doesn't matter. Go out there and work hard.

Trump's response to the young woman is positive thinking at its best. Now apply Trump's mindset principles to your life.

There is a Trump mindset, and you can apply the same principles Trump uses to such great effect in his own life to your life too.

There are 10 principles to the Trump mindset, each of which I will explain in more detail.

1. **Think big.**

2. **Imagine reality using visualization.**

3. **Treat failure as preparation for success.**

4. **Maintain your momentum.**

5. **Keep your energy high with passion and enthusiasm.**

6. **Focus.**

7. **Keep pushing until you get what you want—do not take no for an answer.**

8. **Think positive.**

9. **Stay informed to recognize opportunity.**

10. **Use affirmations. "Survive until '95."**

Your mindset is the background set of beliefs that you hold about yourself, your capabilities, and the world around you. Your mindset determines how you will respond to challenges and struggles, successes and failures, whether you know it or not.

Carol Dweck, a researcher of human potential who popularized the word mindset, divided mindset into two categories: fixed and growth. People with a fixed mindset believe that talent is innate. If you fail, it's because you don't have the necessary talent. You don't have whatever success takes, and you never will. Those with a growth mindset, on the other hand, recognize that failure is something that usually happens on the way to success. Dweck's research showed that individuals with a growth mindset worked harder, and eventually had more success in life, than individuals with a fixed mindset.

The important thing to understand is that you have the ability to choose which mindset will rule your life, fixed or growth. You can choose to view yourself as lacking talent and just not having what it takes, which is how everyone is tempted to feel whenever we face a setback. Or you can choose to view setbacks, and even terrible problems, as opportunities to test yourself and prove that you can survive the challenge. You can either try to avoid pain or recognize that pain leads to growth of both your mind and your spirit. Remember, mindset is a *choice*.

Donald Trump Has a Growth Mindset

The single best way to see whether a person has a fixed mindset or a growth mindset is to look at how he responds to failure. It's easy to feel as if you have a strong and positive mindset when you're winning. It's when you lose that your core mindset reveals itself. When life unexpectedly hands you a setback, or you meet with failure, it is tempting to resign yourself to fate. I often hear men who have failed at an objective say, "Well, I guess I just wasn't good enough." That sort of statement is indicative of a fixed mindset, as it is an assumption that that failure is an end in itself rather than the mark of a new beginning and also implies that the man will never be any better in the future.

Trump often shares his views on mindset on Twitter, telling others, "Sometimes we do things to build up experience and stamina to prepare, but it's to prepare us for something bigger." The mindset revealed in that single 140-character message is both deep and powerful. It should be obvious that Trump's reason for tweeting that was that he, or someone he knew, had recently suffered some kind of setback or loss, and he was reminding them—or perhaps himself—that the experience would help them successfully meet future challenges.

Instead of viewing a loss as the end of the road, Trump's growth mindset should encourage you to look at failure as something that provides you with more experience and stamina, as something that prepares you for bigger opportunities still to come in your future.

> *I like thinking big. I always have. To me it's very simple: if you're going to be thinking anyway, you might as well think big.*
>
> —Donald Trump

These days, most of us spend most of our time simply trying to find a way to keep our heads above water. We're not trying to make it big, we're just trying to pay the bills and make just enough to get by. Part of this is due to changing economic circumstances in America, and part of this is due to our poor education system. Students are taught to dutifully recite facts and figures in school, but how many students are taught how to think big? Who is teaching young men to "go west" these days?

No one, except Donald Trump.

Trump got his start in real estate under his father. Fred Trump owned multi-unit properties in Brooklyn, and he was highly successful. Most people would have been thrilled to just take over the family business and run it, but Trump does not think like most people. He wanted to make big moves into the Manhattan real estate market, because Manhattan is the most cut-throat and financially advanced market in history of Man. He wanted to win, and win big, on the biggest stage of them all.

When he was young, Trump would take long walks and imagine the huge buildings he'd build. As anyone who has been to New York and seen Trump Tower can attest, the Trump buildings have a unique look. They are far more elegant—some would say more extravagant—than all the other buildings on their block.

Trump Tower in New York is loaded with gold-coated guard rails, and the walls and floors are covered in pink Italian marble. There's a fountain that falls from the fourth floor of the public lobby to the ground level. Water tumbles down that gorgeous pink marble, creating a repetitive, soothing sound from the fountain that fits perfectly with the soft beauty of the wall. When you visit the Louvre, in Paris, you'll see the similarities between classic French elegance and Trump's interior design. And yet, there is no other building in the world—inside or out—like Trump Tower.

It wasn't enough for Trump to build the same buildings as his father in Brooklyn, and it wasn't enough for Trump to build the same types of buildings that everyone else in Manhattan was building. Trump wanted more. He thought big, and because of that his architectural legacy will live on for centuries.

So, start thinking about how to think big in your own life. You don't need to think about how to become a billionaire real estate developer, because your situation is different than Donald Trump's. You're not starting with a real estate company in Brooklyn. Thinking big is relative to your situation and how you define reality. For example, I'm a writer without any employees. Now, I could hire people to write for me like James Patterson does and publish ten times more books than I do, or go on the professional speaking circuit, but for me, thinking big means having huge amounts of personal freedom. If I want to go on a hiking trip to Alaska or South Africa, I have no need to delegate any tasks or check up on my employees and their managers. I simply hop on a plane and leave.

Thinking big for me is different than thinking big is for Donald Trump. My personal definition of thinking big is thinking about how I can maximize my personal freedom. I don't want to be a leader or an owner. Remember, leadership is not just power and influence, it is also a burden and a massive responsibility. Ownership ties you down, both to things and people. So, your idea of thinking big may be anything from becoming the CEO of a huge company or having a huge family with 12 kids. Whatever it is, you have the right to define your own reality. Be creative with your definition of what "big" means to you and don't feel the need to justify it to anyone else.

You can think big in any way you choose. Maybe you want large amounts of personal space and free time, or maybe you want to develop a computer game of gargantuan scale, or maybe thinking big just means being able to spend 24 hours a day with your family instead of 12. Thinking big is always relative to your personal definitions and ambitions.

The key here is to stop thinking like an average schlub. Far too many people waste away their lives in front of a television set, or fail to take any risks, and find themselves lamenting when it's too late to change that, "I could have been a contender." Don't could have been. Be. Try. Do. Today.

As with mindset, thinking big is a choice. Trump himself has said as much, "Anyone can think big. The most important thing is the size of your thinking. How big you think determines how big a success you become."

You are what you think you are. Most people think too
little of themselves and devalue their own abilities.

—Donald Trump

Our identities are limited only by our imaginations and the words we use to describe ourselves. Most people think of themselves as being small, average, or irrelevant. But how you think of yourself, and how you define yourself, is a choice you make in the moment.

Where does your definition of self come from? Most of us never ask ourselves that question. Once we do, we usually realize that our view of ourselves has largely come from outside forces, from parents, teachers, peers, the media, or sometimes even society in general. And yet, why should we passively accept a definition of ourselves that was imposed on us by others, without our knowledge or consent?

Since someone is going to tell you what you will think of yourself, that person may as well be you. As Trump observed, "We all have self-definitions. Give yourself a big definition."

You might assume that creating a big identity was easy for Trump, and that it will be hard for you, until you consider the fact that Trump felt the need to apply the very mindset principles you are learning to his own life when he was younger. Just like you, Trump had to start from the beginning; the man he is now is not the same as the young man he once was. The man he is now is the man that he chose to become. "The real reason I wanted out of my father's business," he explained "was that I had loftier dreams and visions."

Of course you might be wondering how you can imagine your own reality. Imagination is a concept that we associate with daydreaming. To imagine reality, begin using visualization techniques.

Once Trump moved to Manhattan, he "began to talk the streets in a way you never do if you just come in town to visit or do business. I got to know all the good properties." As Trump walked the streets, he began to see in his mind's eye what empty lots and dilapidated buildings could be refurbished or torn down and rebuilt.

Trump would walk the streets of undeveloped property and imagine what grand structures he could create. He'd even imagine the type of person who would enjoy living in those same properties. "Trump Tower is a building the critics were skeptical about before it was built, but which the public obviously liked. I'm not talking about the sort of person who inherited money 175 years ago and lives on 84th Street and Park Ave. I'm talking about the wealthy Italian with the beautiful wife and the red Ferrari."

Trump's father has a family business in Brooklyn, which Trump left early in his 20s as he had "loftier dreams and visions." Trump started off as a nobody in Manhattan. How did Trump go from a nobody to a somebody? He'd spend hours walking through Manhattan looking at underdeveloped properties and empty lots. He'd obsess over the possibilities of the area while "dreaming what could be built there."

If you can't see something in person, or in your mind's eye, then you cannot create it.

You must imagine your own dream reality and idea life. You want to be able to see, taste, feel, smell, and touch this life. Your visions should be vivid, and you should focus on this vision when you wake up and before you go to sleep.

Some might ask how a vision is different from a daydream. The difference between daydreamers and visionaries is that visionaries take action each day to bring themselves one step closer to their vision. Visionaries also recognize that, as Trump said, it may take 30 years for your vision to become reality.

How can you begin to visualize success? Here is an exercise comes from my bestselling mindset book, *Gorilla Mindset*. You begin with the Perfect Day.

After reading this paragraph, close your eyes. Using the power of your mind, think about where you would wake up tomorrow, if you lived in a perfect world. Yes, of course, it will take years to create your perfect world. But for now, you are only thinking about what is possible. Who do you wake up next to? Where do you wake up? Imagine the scenery. If you're by an ocean, hear the waves crashing against the surface of the beach. Smell the salt water. Feel the sunshine coming into your room.

As you create your life vision, meditate on it each night before bed. You have now set your life vision.

Each day you wake up, ask yourself if you are living in a way that will bring you closer to your life vision. Hold yourself accountable for your thoughts and emotions, in each and every passing moment.

If you this sounds too abstract to you, consider my own example. Before becoming a bestselling author, I spent years visualizing my perfect life. In my thought exercise, I wake up in a house feeling refreshed. My house is full of love. I imagined waking up and working from home, earning a living as a professional writer. I imagined my own impact on the culture increasing every year, until reaching a tipping point where I experienced my success each and every day.

Today I live that life that I previously could only imagine. It took me years to reach this point, and each day I express my gratitude to all those who have helped me reach it, to my readers and my fans. I never take anyone for granted, and every day I hold myself accountable to the people who made this life possible.

What is your life vision? What daily mental habits will bring you closer to your vision? Who will help you achieve your dreams? What are you doing today to meet those people? Are you providing value to the world each day, which is what it takes to live your life vision? These are real questions that you must answer every day. As you get into the habit of asking and answering these questions, you'll find that the limits to your willpower begin to fade away. You spend less time on distractions and less energy on destructive and dramatic people. You begin to see your vision take shape with increasingly clear and powerful focus.

Sheer persistence is the difference between success and failure.

—Donald Trump

No matter how great you are, no matter how talented you are, sooner or later you are going to encounter failure in life. Even the greatest athletes miss most of the shots they take. In baseball, failing to reach first base 6 out of 10 times will make you a Hall of Famer. The greatest basketball player of all time, Michael Jordan, missed more than 50 percent of the field goals he attempted in his career. Most people let failure get to them and bring them down much too easily. Most people are far too ready to define themselves as a failure.

Do you know the difference between a winner and a loser? It's not the mere fact of losing a contest. Everyone loses eventually, winners and losers alike. Everyone has experienced defeat and everyone has failed at something. The difference is that winners keep going and they find new challenges in life until they find success. That's why winning or losing is less of a discrete life outcome and more of a mindset. When you refuse to accept defeat by pushing forward and moving on instead of giving up, you make yourself into a winner.

How you deal with failure is a choice you must make. You can view failure as the end of the road. You can view it as "game over". That is exactly how quitters and losers think.

But it is far more powerful to view failure as a step forward in the process of success, as an experience preparing you for something great. Failing at something means that you tried it, and even if you didn't succeed, you became stronger as a result. You learned from it. You are better prepared for life.

With every failure you will learn more life skills.

Scott Adams has a saying: "Fail fast." He knows what he's talking about. He's failed before. But every successful person has failed in some way, at some point. So fail fast, move on to the next thing, and get over it.

When you find yourself starting to get down on yourself due to failure, always remember that you are preparing for something bigger and better. Many people do not hit their big break until later in life. That is really another way of saying that they work hard in obscurity for years, or even decades, before their hard work pays off. Successful people often joke that it takes at least ten years to become an overnight success.

Chances are you've watched or heard of *A Game of Thrones*, a hit HBO series based on a popular series of epic fantasy novels. But I bet you do not know that its author, George R.R. Martin, was not a successful author for most of his life. He never had a bestseller until writing *A Song of Fire and Ice*. Martin did not receive any mainstream acclaim as a writer until he reached his fifties, and he did not get really big until he was in his sixties.

Think about that. Imagine if George R.R. Martin had quit writing books at 45 because he failed to write a bestseller. If Martin had quit in middle-age, he'd never have become a massively successful author, and we would not have his books and his television series to enjoy.

J.K. Rowling spent six years writing *Harry Potter and the Philosopher's Stone*. It was rejected by nine publishers before Bloomsbury

Publishing offered her a book contract. Now that book alone has sold 107 million copies, and the rest of the series has sold over 300 million copies. Imagine if Rowling had quit after receiving her eighth rejection!

"Life," as Mark Twain said, "is less of a dance and more of a wrestling match." Sometimes you win and sometimes life pins you. You can view yourself as getting stronger from this wrestling match with life, or you can choose to feel defeated. If you treat a failure as a major defeat, you can become bitter like so many people are these days.

By choosing to view your failures in life as preparations for something great, you are setting yourself up to live a long-term life with a vision for success.

Treat failure as an unpleasant, but necessary step toward something bigger, and you will grow stronger each day, even on those days when you feel like you're struggling.

> *I have devoted a lot of time to studying and applying the power of momentum to my own life and business. I do not ever want to lose my momentum. The lesson applies whether you are in real estate or not.*

—Donald Trump

In life you are either moving forward or backwards. It is impossible to remain still, because even if we do not move, time will pass us by. Although we think of ourselves as the center of the universe, the world will keep moving with or without us. Time waits for no man. That includes Trump, that includes you, and that includes me.

Donald Trump's biggest personal and professional setback occurred in the 1990s. The real estate market crashed. Trump wasn't prepared for the possibility of a crash, and he had even personally guaranteed the debt on many of the properties. When he was asked why he found himself struggling, Trump was candid.

According to Trump, he had stopped moving forward and stopped pushing. He had begun to view himself as a success and he thought he could stop working hard. He began enjoying his wealth and status, spending more of his time gallivanting with women and partying than on building his business. He had started thinking in terms of protecting what he had rather than building onto it. It was a lesson Trump would not forget again.

After making a successful return from his setbacks in the 90s, Trump has been unstoppable. He continued developing hundreds of properties, wrote several best-selling books, and both launched and starred in the highest-rated show on television, *The Apprentice*. While building his businesses, Trump also gave speeches and earned seven-figure speaking fees.

You build and maintain momentum by continually challenging yourself. Once you become a success in one area of your life, it is important to begin developing other skills and learning new talents. As you learn new talents and develop new skills, you will move forward and continue to improve your odds of success across a wider range of activities. Scott Adams, who in addition to being a massively successful cartoonist and bestselling author is also a formidable mindset teacher, has said, "Each skill you learn doubles your odds of success."

This book you're reading has already improved your mindset skill set. Yes, mindset is a skill, and an important one at that. Mindset involves improving your thinking, becoming more optimistic, and developing control over your emotions. As you improve your skills in the mindset area, you'll find other areas of your life improve as a result. You will be more assertive in business meetings and in your career. You will not be afraid to stand up for yourself. At the same time, you will be more calm and composed under pressure because you understand how to keep things in perspective. You will not freak out at the possibility of failure or crack under stress.

Remember that your mindset will become stronger and you will become more focused and determined on the basis of the challenges you undertake and the growth you subsequently experience. Don't hesitate to challenge yourself!

Wherever you are in life, you can build your momentum by challenging yourself just a little bit more. You can work for a few minutes a day learning a new skill. You can practice your public speaking in front of a mirror. You can take a short walk or begin a new exercise program.

Each year, I've pushed myself harder. After creating the best men's interest website in the world, I started a podcast which now has a five-star rating, wrote what became the bestselling mindset book, and then built a massive social media account. My Twitter account receives over 50 million page views every month, which is more traffic than many leading news sites enjoy. Did I stop pushing? No, of course not! My next step was to produce an important documentary on free speech, *Silenced*, after which I started writing the very book you're now reading.

I don't bring up any of this to brag. My goal is to inspire you! Believe me, there is no one who expected me to be able to do *any* of this when I began. Not even me. I had the vision of where I wanted to be, but I had to build my momentum gradually, step-by-step, building gradually on each success and failure alike. Now, in hindsight, it all looks inevitable. But it wasn't. Success is the result of Vision + Momentum.

I didn't do it perfectly. I made mistakes. I imposed unnecessary limits on myself. At times, my thinking wasn't big enough, and I've discovered that too often, when I've done well in a particular area, I tended to start coasting there. So, I've learned from Trump's mistakes and from his victories. You should do the same from mine.

Always challenge yourself. Never rest on past successes because success is always a temporary state. In life, you can never be "successful" in a full-stop, end-of-story way. Life is dynamic, nothing ever stays the same forever. You only experience success in the moment, and living life to the full in the moment requires both movement and momentum.

> *Without momentum there's a lack of energy that can lead the best of ideas to nowhere. Get your momentum going— and keep it going.*

> —Donald Trump

You become high-energy by finding your passion. When you find your passion, you'll actually have trouble not working harder. You'll find it difficult to stop working.

Even if you can't live your passion 24/7, find a few minutes a day to do something that makes you passionate. For some it's a hobby that excites them. For others, it's a pastime that relaxes them.

You want to wake up excited for life and feeling purposeful. Even if you hate your job, focus on the passion of providing for your family. Instead of viewing your job as being a pointless dead-end, recognize that it allows you to live your passion of taking care of the family that you love and that loves you.

Find moments of passion every day. Find something that you look forward to. Remember that mindset changes are often small, but over time, these small changes add up to big effects.

Once you get into the habit of living life with passion and purpose, then your newfound energy will begin to spill over into other areas of your life. Maybe your dead-end job won't seem so dead-end at all. Maybe you'll find the energy to start working on a side business on weekends or after work hours. Or maybe you'll find yourself becoming a better parent, or a better husband or wife.

When you begin adding even a few minutes of passion into your day, you'll soon start to notice big effects.

> *Your destiny is to fulfill those things upon which you focus most intently. So choose to keep your focus on that which is truly magnificent, beautiful, uplifting and joyful. Your life is always moving toward something.*
>
> —Ralph Marston

We often think about our focus as our attention and sometimes we say things like "I can't focus!" This tends to mean you can't concentrate on a task you're doing, or you're procrastinating. Yet there's a deeper meaning to focus, one you've likely never seen before and certainly were not taught in school.

Your focus is related to how you frame, or choose to see, the situations in which you find yourself.

Even when you say "I can't focus!" you are actually focusing. Think about it. When you claim to be unfocused in the present moment, what you are choosing to see, what you are actually focusing on, is how you can't focus. We are actually focused 100 percent of the time. We are always framing our situation. If you're commuting and you're not paying attention to the road, it may be because you're focused on a text message or a daydream or a fight you had with a loved one. You are not unfocused, you are simply focusing on something different than what you should be focusing on.

The reality is that you can only focus on one task at a time. There is only a single frame for any situation. There is no such thing as multi-tasking.

When you feel like you're losing focus, check in with yourself at that moment and talk yourself through it. Focus on your surroundings perhaps by saying to yourself, "OK. I'm sitting at my computer. I'm trying to work but I don't feel like working. Even though I don't feel like working, my job is important to me because it helps me live a better life for myself and my family."

Do you see what you did there? You changed your focus from your on-the-job boredom to what you want to accomplish for your family. You changed your framing of the situation.

If you don't feel like going to the gym, you are often focused on how much exercising hurts or how you can't expect any immediate rewards. That's when you need to change your focus to something more positive. Literally talk to yourself in the present moment about the situation. "All right, I do not feel like going to the gym right now, but I do feel like having more energy and living a longer life. People depend on me and I want to be there for them. Life is a great adventure and I want to be strong and healthy for it."

Again, you are changing your focus from something you don't want to do (hit the gym) to something you do want to do (have more energy and live a better life).

Your life is made up of individual moments, and each moment is defined by your focus. Choose what you focus on, and always be sure to reframe your focus away from problems and toward the benefits you can achieve from dealing with those problems.

> *When faced with a big challenge, do not look at what is, instead focus on what can be.*
>
> —Donald Trump

How you face a problem determines how that problem will control you. We all have the same issues. We have insecurities. We have vulnerabilities. We have strengths and weaknesses. At times, we all feel overwhelmed by life. We question ourselves and wonder if we are good enough.

But rather than accept your current limits, you can challenge them. One of the best ways to challenge your limits is to choose to view your problems as opportunities for personal, spiritual, and emotional growth.

Reframing is another lesson I teach in my book *Gorilla Mindset,* and Donald Trump is a master at reframing. Reframing refers to making a conscious decision to view a challenge or a frustration as an opportunity for growth. Trump speaks of reframing often, advising, "Don't emphasize the problem so much—emphasize the solution. It's a mindset that works."

Most people view problems as something bad. But the fact is that problems can genuinely help you improve and grow. Trump likes to call problems "mind exercises". He says, "See problems as a mind exercise. Enjoy the challenge—and remember to keep focused on your goals."

Keep pushing. Do not take no for an answer.

—Donald Trump

When we hear the word "pushy," we tend to think of the annoying guy or girl who just won't leave us alone. That type of pushy is not what Trump means when he tells people to keep pushing. Pushing, more often than not, means *finding out what the other person wants,* not forcing them to accept what you want. Think about it this way.

Trump pushed his way past 16 other Republican primary challengers by getting his message out to the media. The normal passive way for a political candidate to get his message out is to ask the media to write about him, spam them with daily press releases, and kiss every behind with the potential to fund or otherwise support his campaign. Trump didn't do that. He pushed his message out

himself. He made it impossible to ignore him by using his social media platforms. Trump kept pushing past objections, through media
hoaxes, and bulldozed public campaigns to stop talking about him
by giving the media what it wanted most: an exciting story about a
popular, controversial candidate.

Pushy doesn't sound so bad now, does it? Remember that pushy
isn't just annoying people. If you don't add value, then you're not
pushy, you're simply a parasite looking to get something from someone while providing nothing to them. When you provide value, you
should push your message, product, or service out to the market.
You should push your way to success in a new job or a new business
venture. You should push past objections when closing a sale. Have
confidence in yourself and in the value of what you're offering to
others.

I wanted you to buy this book. But rather than spamming your
email or begging you to buy it, I pushed you into buying it in a
great, mutually beneficial way. I designed an excellent book cover
that would attract your eye. I built up my brand as a mindset expert.
Each and every word on the Amazon description page was carefully
considered and selected. I imagined every objection you could possibly have to buying the book, and I pushed you past them.

You're reading it now, aren't you? So obviously, it works.

So, don't think of being pushy as a bad thing, so long as you are
providing value along the way.

Pushing is really just another way of moving forward. In life
you must keep pushing forward, even when there are obstacles in
your way. Obstacles present themselves in many forms. Sometimes
you are stuck in a bad job, a bad relationship, or you have a health
problem.

I've dealt with all three in the past. For example, due to a side
effect from a medication that doctors prescribed me, I developed

Red Skin Syndrome. It was truly horrible. My body ached and I couldn't get out of bed. Huge patches of skin across my body turned bright red, and the pain was worse than any sunburn I had ever had. My hair began to fall out and I was about as miserable as I could be.

While I was suffering through Red Skin Syndrome, there was a choice for me to make. As long as you are conscious, there is always a choice. I had two choices. I could give up, stop moving and let the syndrome keep me down until it went away. Or, I could keep pushing.

Now pushing forward is always relative. It means something very different when you are healthy and feeling good than when you are in pain and bedridden. I pushed myself out of bed to walk down one flight of stairs and then back up again, as at first, that was all my body could take. The next day, I walked down two flights of stairs. After a couple of weeks, I could leave my house and walk around the block. Eventually my body was back in shape, although the dreadful skin condition persisted for nearly four more years. Even today my skin will occasionally break out into a horrible rash. But now, it doesn't even slow me down.

I pushed through it. And you can push through whatever challenge faces you.

Keep pushing for the job you want. Push for the body you want. Push for the health and the relationships you want. Push yourself forward.

Yes, sometimes you need things from other people. Pushing doesn't mean annoying them until they give it to you. When you need something from someone, find a way to deliver value to them. Often, the best way to push through a barrier with another person is to find out what they want and help them get it.

Push yourself hard and you'll begin to live the Trump mindset.

*Formulate and stamp indelibly on your mind a mental
picture of yourself as succeeding. Hold this picture tena-
ciously. Never permit it to fade. Your mind will seek to
develop the picture.... Do not build up obstacles in your
imagination.*

—Norman Vincent Peale,
The Power of Positive Thinking

The truth about life is that it's both a beautiful adventure and
a terrifying experience full of self-doubt and uncertainty. You can
choose to dwell on the negative aspects of life or you can change
your focus to the positive aspects of life. For example, we tend to
view self-doubt as a horrible problem to have, and it can be. Yet you
can choose to think differently about your self-doubt. You can view
self-doubt as a challenge. You can look at it as something to overcome. You can tell yourself, "All right, my self-doubt is problem,
but it's amazing that through regular practice and mindset training,
I *will* be able to eliminate it. Imagine how great I'm going to feel
by defeating this challenge and gaining new confidence in myself!"

What you're doing is using the power of positive thinking. Positive thinking does not mean you live in a state of denial. It doesn't
mean you deny reality or pretend you're in a different situation than
you are. Positive thinking means that you recognize that life has
pluses and minuses, and that part of the beautiful journey of life is
learning how to overcome the negative aspects.

After all, how else can you you grow physically, emotionally, and
spiritually? Yes, I used the word spiritual. We live in a spiritually
bankrupt time where people have little hope for the future and lack
a belief in themselves. Spiritual growth tends to go hand in hand
with positive thinking, as staring into the abyss seldom improves
anyone's state of mind.

When you start from the bottom, you are not a loser, as many people think. In fact, starting from the bottom means that you *cannot* lose. It means you have *unlimited* upside potential. Believe it or not, in many ways making it to the top is less exciting than climbing up the first rung of the ladder. Once you make it in life, (and remember, you'll never truly make it, since life has a way of throwing unavoidable new challenges at even the most successful individuals) you tend to take fewer risks as you have more to lose. When you're starting off at the bottom, at any age, you can afford to take more risks. You can be bolder and more audacious. You can think bigger.

Now, do you see what I just did there? I used the power of positive thinking to change how you feel about starting off from the bottom with nothing. You might have even started to feel sorry for those poor rich people, worrying about easy it would be for them to lose it all as they spend their days imagining the worst instead of looking ahead to a bigger, better future. Positive thinking is a powerful way to reliably turn negatives into positives.

Some people are skeptical of positive thinking, but what do you have to lose? When people tell me that they don't believe me about its benefits, my answer is always to perform a thought experiment based on the assumption I am wrong.

If you believe positive thinking doesn't work, you'll wake up every day believing that life is limited. You'll miss out on opportunities in front of you because you're not looking for them. Your life and your relationships will stagnate because the everyday challenges of your life will seem too difficult to change, let alone improve. Your outlook will be fatalistic, as everything appears beyond your control, so putting effort into anything will be futile.

Now imagine you believe that positive thinking works. You wake up in a bad mood and feel like you're going to have one of those days. Rather than passively accept the sort of crappy day that we all have from time to time, you take an active approach to managing your day. You open yourself to possibilities. You remind yourself that life has endless possibilities, and everywhere you look you see opportunities. Your own mind and consciousness begin to expand. You can see a broad range of options in front of you. Suddenly you believe life has purpose in meaning.

Every day you are alive, you face a single, specific choice, and every day it's the most important decision you have to make. You can choose to believe that today, for whatever reason, your life doesn't matter and there is nothing you can do about it. Or you can choose to apply the power of positive thinking to your life.

Look, you've *tried* negative thinking. We all have. Many of us, perhaps most of us, were raised in environments where people rarely praised us and criticized us all the time. And you know where it will get you, which is nowhere.

So why not try positive thinking? After all, you have nothing to lose but bad habits, bad moods, and bad outcomes.

> *Keep stimulating your mind with big ideas. Be a collector of big ideas. Constantly fill your mind with new information, and use this new information to spawn new ideas. Put these ideas together to create big ideas for solving problems, for making money, for getting things done faster and cheaper, and for making complex things simple.*
>
> —Donald Trump

By now you're realizing that mindset, thinking big, thinking positive, and visualization are not abstract concepts. You've seen how Trump applied them to his life, and now you know how to apply them to your own life.

Creating the life of your dreams requires you to remain connected to the outside world. If you don't study history and current cultural trends, you'll be blindsided by life again and again. You'll also miss out on amazing business and personal opportunities.

Trump begins each day by reading five newspapers and checking social media to see what happened overnight. He also talks to real Americans. He doesn't limit his interactions to the rich and famous like most celebrities do. Two decades ago Trump suggested talking to cab drivers: "When I'm in another city and I take a cab, I'll always make it a point to ask the cab driver questions. I ask and I ask and I ask until I begin to get a gut feeling about something." While Trump probably hasn't taken a cab in many years, you can bet he uses the same principles when talking to his security detail, his barber, and other regular Americans he encounters in daily life.

Regular Americans like cab drivers and waiters aren't just ordinary people. They are your fellow citizens, and they have their own perspective on the world. Ask them to share it with you and you will often be surprised by what you learn. No matter where I travel, whether I'm in Europe, or Asia, or the Americas, I make it a point to talk to everyone I encounter and ask them questions.

However there is a risk to remaining connected. We often use knowledge, and the need to acquire it, as a way to rationalize our procrastination. Do not become a social media addict or information junkie who always researches and never takes action. We think we are waiting for that perfect bit of information before we can act. We think if we can only create the perfect strategy, we will succeed. But remember the section on momentum. Momentum requires movement, and movement requires action. So stay connected, study the trends, and then use those trends by taking action in your own life.

Trump followed his own advice this election. He previously

told his readers and listeners: "Take advantage of big trends. Many events that occur appear surprising to most people but are really quite inevitable and predictable."

Before running for President, Trump had his staff spend a lot of time listening to talk radio. He wanted to understand the issues that were impacting real Americans. Trump learned about some of the biggest threats facing America, and he used this knowledge to run the most successful primary campaign in political history, a campaign so unexpected that none of the professionals predicted it. A victorious campaign that almost no one besides me, Scott Adams, and Vox Day saw coming.

So spend time each day, preferably early in the day, connecting to the outside world.

Study your industry too. For example, my industry is writing and publishing. No author can make it just being a writer. Anyone can write. But being a successful writer requires understanding publishing trends, studying the market, and writing books that readers want to not only read, but own.

This very book you're reading is the result of my study of trends in the publishing world and in the mainstream media. I noticed that the media pundits always flailed cluelessly about whenever they discussed Trump. They couldn't understand his success, they had no idea what he was doing, and yet their terrible analyses would draw record page views and viewers, because people wanted to understand Trump. People always want to understand success.

After talking to literally tens of thousands of people, both in person and online, I was able to write the perfect Trump book. This book is the direct result of me staying connected to you, my friendly readers.

Your own industry has trends. Every industry does. There are new businesses and new organizations being formed in every industry around the world each day. How will you use your knowledge of big trends in the world around you to make big moves in your own life? That is not a rhetorical question. Ask it and answer it to the best of your ability every day.

> Start every day thinking, "Today is a great day. I live in the greatest nation on earth. I have a great profession. It is great to be alive. There are plenty of opportunities for me to be successful today."

> —Donald Trump, *Think Big and Kick Ass*

You spend hours each day talking to yourself. This running conversation is known as your inner monologue, and mastering it is essential to your mindset success. A powerful way to take control of your inner monologue is by using affirmations when you talk to yourself.

An affirmation can be thought of as a message that persuades you to believe in yourself. A big part of mindset is persuading yourself to think positively and to avoid letting life's challenges get you down. Scott Adams called Trump "a master persuader", and when you consider that mindset is a form of persuasion, you see why Trump uses affirmations. Trump is persuading *himself* of the things he needs to believe in order to accomplish his vision.

Trump's positive affirmation mentioned above is absolutely true. Today *is* a great day. Each and every single day is a once-in-a-lifetime opportunity to grow and to overcome challenges. You will only live today once. Live it well. Live it great!

If you don't believe me when I say that today is great, talk to older people with regrets about how much time they feel they wasted. Most of us don't know what we have until it's gone, and that's just as true of our time on this earth as it is of our possessions and our relationships.

Affirmations can also be used to overcome personal struggles. Trump faced a serious professional crisis in the 1990s. He was on the brink of losing it all. How did he stay focused?

What he did was to state a daily affirmation: "Survive 'til 95!" Trump knew that if he could keep his businesses open until 1995, then the terrible real estate crisis would be over and he would be able to recover. Whenever he felt frustrated, or even afraid, Trump would return to his powerful words of affirmation. Survive until '95!

Needless to say, he not only survived until 1995, he has thrived since then.

Trump is not the only successful person to use affirmations. Gawker Media, a collection of vile clickbait sites, a company which had a history of destroying people's lives, published revenge porn starring champion wrestler and entertainer Hulk Hogan. Hogan sued Gawker, which was owned by the rich and powerful British entrepreneur Nick Denton.

Even a strong case is stressful, as litigation drags on. During the trial, Denton proved to be an arrogant and intimidating man, who even managed to "scare the hell" out of Hogan, according to the *New York Post*. And believe it or not, Hogan used affirmations during his lawsuit against Gawker.

> *Asked how he stayed strong through the trial, Hogan said, "All I did was write for 11 days affirmations: 'I am victorious. I am grateful. I am highly favored by God and His universe.'" Ultimately, a Florida jury awarded him $65 million for emotional distress, $50 million for damage to his career and another $25 million to punish the defendants.*
>
> —"Hulk Hogan and Nick Denton had a sex tape trial 'stare-down'", Julia Marsh, *The New York Post*

Scott Adams, the world-famous creator of *Dilbert*, is famous for using affirmations. He has even written about them in a book called *The Dilbert Future*.

> *The idea behind writing affirmations is that you simply write down your goals 15 times a day and somehow, as if by magic, coincidences start to build until you achieve your objective against all odds. Prior to my Dilbert success, I used affirmations on a string of hugely unlikely goals that all materialized in ways that seemed miraculous. Some of the successes you can explain away by assuming I'm hugely talented and incredibly sexy, and therefore it is no surprise that I accomplished my goals despite seemingly long odds. But some of my goals involved neither hard work nor skill of any kind. I succeeded with those too, against all odds. Those are harder to explain, at least for me, since the most common explanation is that they are a delusion. I found my experience with affirmations fascinating and puzzling, and so I wrote about it.*

One inexplicably powerful use of affirmations is recounted in Kamal Ravikant's book, *Love Yourself Like Your Life Depends on It*. Kamal was struck with a mysterious illness that nearly killed him. No medical remedy was available and it seemed hopeless. But Kamal began looking into the mirror and saying, "I love you." He'd say this several times each day, and sometimes he would even smile while saying it. His statement, his love for himself, was a powerful affirmation that saved his life. In time, Kamal's health returned.

Now, there is no science behind what Kamal did, and "I love you" would not be an affirmation that would work for me. Maybe it would work for you, more likely it would not. You must tailor your mindset affirmations for yourself. What works for you, Scott

Adams, Donald Trump, Kamal Ravikant, Hulk Hogan, or Mike
Cernovich will almost always be different, because we all have different visions for our life.

I am Too Big to Ignore

It probably won't surprise you to know that I use affirmations in my
own life. It takes a lot of energy and enthusiasm to accomplish what
I do, especially since the mainstream media attacks me regularly. My
daily mantra is this: "I will become too big to ignore."

There are two parts to my affirmation. The first is "I WILL." Life
does not wait for you. Time will pass you by. Merely showing up is
not enough. I must WILL whatever it is that I want into existence.
This was especially true for me, as a kid who grew up poor, fat, and
bullied.

Becoming "too big to ignore" is a powerful message for me,
because I am building my own media platforms and even self-
published my own best-selling books. I don't need permission to
be on television, to work for a news website, or to write for a newspaper. I am my own media. I am, as I have repeatedly affirmed, too
big to ignore!

Why is being ignored something of particular meaning to me?
Because it would be delusional to think I can achieve my life vision
without the help of others. Yes, others *must* pay attention to me
and my writing, or else I'll have zero influence and I certainly won't
succeed as an author. That is why the mainstream media does its
best to try to ignore me when they can and minimize me when they
can't.

But it won't work. I *will* become too big to ignore. And some of
you are reading this book because that affirmation is already coming
to pass.

My life vision is to work for myself, and when starting a media empire from scratch, you absolutely need to be noticed by your future readers and viewers. To keep myself focused, and to overcome any self-doubt or fear of failure, I persuade myself of that same message. I will become too big to ignore.

Your Mindset Will Vary

You have your own mindset. You have your own vision. Your own affirmation has to be unique to you because your vision is not mine. Only you know what your vision is. Only you can create the right affirmation for yourself. Make it personal, make it *powerful*, and make sure it is *directly* related to your goals and to your life vision.

Remember that all of Trump's mindset principles tie closely together. An affirmation is thinking big (principle 1), uses positive thinking (principle 8), is based on your life vision (principle 8), and directs your focus (point 6) to your life vision.

What is your vision? That is the single most important question you must answer. And once you know the answer, you can begin the process of making yourself great.

Part 4: Conclusion

The Rise of Trump

The rise of Trump has been fascinating to watch, and I thank you for reading my own observations on it. The show it has offered us has been like nothing else we will see in our lifetimes. The education we have been presented has been incomparable. You will now recognize where the culture in the U.S. and broader West is heading. Unlike all the political pundits and so-called experts, you get it.

More than that, you have learned valuable lessons from Trump's example. You understand the power of positive thinking. You know how to develop a dominant mindset, and you understand how to use A/B tests to improve your life. You no longer fear failure, because you recognize that failure merely represents deeper knowledge about the world you have obtained.

Like Donald Trump, you are now ready to live life on *your* terms.

To take your mindset to the next level, I encourage you to read my #1 bestselling book on mindset: *Gorilla Mindset: How to Control Your Thoughts and Emotions to Live Life on Your Terms*. Although it was originally written with men in mind, many women have thanked me for helping them live more powerful lives with *Gorilla Mindset*.

My book of essays, *Danger & Play* also shows you how to develop a more dominant mindset, improve your health, and generally kick ass at life.

You can also follow my writing at DangerAndPlay.com, which has been read by millions of people. Be forewarned, however. DangerAndPlay publishes the edgiest articles online, as it takes no prisoners and spares no sacred cows.

CPSIA information can be obtained
at www.ICGtesting.com
Printed in the USA
BVOW10s0749130417
481064BV00008B/121/P